LAWS
of
LOVE

LAWS
of
LOVE

Margaret Pounders

UNITY® Books

Unity Village, Missouri

Second Edition 2000

To receive a catalog of all Unity publications (books, cassettes, compact discs, and magazines) or to place an order, call Customer Service Department: (816) 969-2069 or 1-800-669-0282.

The publisher wishes to acknowledge the editorial work of Raymond Teague, Michael Maday, and Medini Longwell; the copy services of Kay Thomure, Deborah Dribben, and Beth Anderson; the production help of Rozanne Devine and Jane Blackwood; and the marketing efforts of Allen Liles, Jenee Meyer, and Sharon Sartin.

Cover design by Gretchen West

Cover photo by Martin Barraud © 1998–1999 TONY STONE IMAGES

Interior design by Coleridge Design

Photo of author by © 1999 Glamour Shots

LLC 99-66955
ISBN 0-87159-254-1
Canada BN 13252 9033 RT

Contents

Introduction

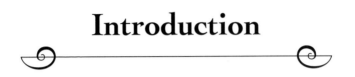

"Love is the fulfilling of the law."[1]

"Let us have faith, Mr. President, that the Lord is on our side," the chaplain admonished Abraham Lincoln during the early days of the Civil War.

"I am not concerned with that," Lincoln quietly replied, "for I know that the Lord is always on the side of right. My prayer is that I and this country be on the Lord's side."

Successfully getting "on the Lord's side" and staying there is a lesson few people learn in a lifetime; yet this is the only way to Truth, the Truth that God plays no favorites. Everyone is God's favorite. God's love is equal for the just and the unjust, the wise and the simple, the rich and the poor, the healthy and the sick. Because we try, consciously or otherwise, to go against God's laws of love, it sometimes seems to us that God plays favorites. Nothing could be further from the Truth because, while God is love—personal and indwelling, God is also law—perfect and immutable. Though Spirit, the life essence of each one of us, loves us with a love beyond human comprehension, this same Spirit is Principle, eternal and unchanging.

The small child approaches the stove. Many times her mother has warned: "Hot! Mustn't touch!" Curious, the child reaches out a finger to test it; then, with a loud yelp, quickly withdraws. She has learned an instant lesson in the law of cause and effect, a lesson she will never forget.

Jim, a man I know, constantly harbors unhappy thoughts. "What's the world coming to?" is Jim's favorite expression. He listens to cries on the radio of dishonesty in government; he watches tales of violence on his television set; he reads in the newspapers of financial disasters. His conversations concern the things that "they" say: "Prices are rising." "It's going around." "There's sure to be an epidemic!" "Depression!" "War!"

With no understanding or realization of what he is doing, Jim gathers about himself seemingly insignificant particles of negativity. These colonies of dark brown thought-substance have an affinity for thoughts of like nature. These invisible parasites group together and sap the strength from their host. Then they attack him at his most vulnerable point—perhaps a physical organ, perhaps his pocketbook, perhaps his relationships with others.

It is easy for the child to see the correlation between fire and pain. It takes more insight to see the connection between Jim's suffering and the thoughts he has nourished for years.

Jim will likely consult a physician, a financial counselor, or a psychiatrist. He will receive medication, advice, perhaps surgery. His condition may improve . . . for a while. But no medication, no advice, no surgery will cure him permanently. He will still have a sick body, sick emotions, and sick relationships until he rids himself of his sick thoughts.

If God is love, as we have been taught since

childhood, why does God not intervene and save Jim and others like him from their plights?

In the same way we can ask: Why does the law of mathematics not intervene and make two plus two equal five for the convenience of the child who failed to study for his exam? Why do the principles of music not eradicate the disharmony that results when F natural is substituted for F sharp in the key of G?

Plato called God a "geometrician."[2] The astronomer Sir James Jeans described God as "an infinite thinker, thinking mathematically."[3]

Emerson wrote: "The law holds with equal sureness of all right action. Love and you shall be loved. All love is mathematically just, as much as the two sides of an algebraic equation."[4]

Charles Fillmore taught: "Love, in Divine Mind, is the idea of universal unity. In expression, love is the power that joins and binds in divine harmony the universe and everything in it."[5]

The laws of the universe, like the laws of music and mathematics, know only how to be. Their use or misuse is up to us, as creatures of free will.

Though Jesus told us, "With God all things are possible,"[6] never did he imply that God alters

His laws to comply with our desires. "With God," we are in accord with God's perfect plan for our life. "With God," we understand and consciously align ourselves with the principles through which the universe operates. "With God," every power in the universe is at our disposal.

A man stands in the sunshine with a bag covering his head. Though he is deprived of the sunshine for a time, the natural disintegration of the bag will eventually allow the sun to break through and shine upon him. Or he can simply remove the bag and bask in the sun's life-giving rays.

We have the same choice. We cannot break the law. We can only break ourselves by attempting to do so.

These twelve chapters do not purport to contain all God's laws. Just as there are but seven spectral colors reflecting an infinite variety of combinations and shades, in Truth there is but one law—love—expressing in a myriad of ways. These chapters tell only some of those ways.

The section "Equations" looks at the attitudes of mind best described by Paul when he said, "Do not be deceived; God is not mocked, for whatever a man sows, that he will also reap."[7]

These laws are most readily recognized. "Paradoxes" deals with those laws which to human thinking seem illogical. To be understood, they must be viewed from a higher vantage point. Many of Jesus' greatest teachings, such as the Sermon on the Mount and many of his parables, are paradoxical to human thought. In "Spirals," we examine the natural tendency of life to express in ever-expanding and evolving modes. "Transcendencies" are laws beyond those that we perceive with the five physical senses. They are gifts that the soul alone beholds.

Each concept—equation, paradox, spiral, transcendency—brings us back to the inescapable truth that love inevitably wins out. It can come to pass through suffering, trial and error, and painful tribulation. Or, like removing a bag from our head, we can simply toss aside the burdensome false concepts and through understanding and practice, let the law instruct us in its life-sustaining lessons of love; for truly, "Love is the fulfilling of the law."

All the examples I have used in this book are factual. However, names, except for those well known, have been changed.

EQUATIONS

Chapter 1

Patterns

⟳————————————⟲

"For as he thinketh in his heart, so is he." [1]

The ant busily carried his morsel of food from the end of my self-made sandpile into the hollowed mound where he and his colony made their home. Why, I wondered, watching in fascination, was he an ant and I a human? I stroked Snowball's soft, black fur as she purred contentedly at my side. What force had created her a cat and me a child? A rooster crowed proudly. What if I had been given the body of a chicken, instead of that of a little girl? The implications were awesome!

"Cats and ants and chickens have no souls," my Sunday school teacher confidently explained a few days later. Never had I heard anything so ridiculous.

"Snowball does!" I insisted.

"No," Mrs. Higgins indulgently replied, "only people have souls." How did she know? I pondered as I watched her tape on the bulletin board a drawing of Abraham preparing to sacrifice his son Isaac.

Myrtle Fillmore, cofounder with her husband Charles of the Unity movement, may have had similar thoughts. She had been told by doctors that she had only a few months to live; yet her life extended forty-five years beyond this "death sentence." Describing her healing for *Unity Magazine*, she wrote:

> Life is everywhere—in worm and in man. "Then why does not the life in the worm make a body like man's?" I asked. Then I thought, "The worm has not as much sense as man." Ah! intelligence, as well as life, is needed to make a body.[2]

Life . . . intelligence. "Build thee more stately mansions; O my soul," wrote the poet,[3] knowing that consciousness precisely weaves for itself a suitable dwelling place, a temple fit for its destiny. Our body is not merely a group of atoms drawn together through some chance encounter; rather, it is the outer manifestation of our individuality, the composite of all we think, all we feel, all we are.

The soul, the life essence in all its multiplicity of forms, builds to whatever level it is called upon to express. If only a small amount of expression is necessary, then the body need not be unduly intricate. In the case of humans, with our limitless capacity for expression, a suitable instrument has been provided, one with the potential for expression far beyond that which we now use. If we desire to express a better body, we can; and the key to this expression is in the expansion of our consciousness.

Truth Vs. Fact

The expansion of the consciousness begins with an understanding of the difference between Truth and fact. Truth is absolute, unchanging, eternal. Truth is intangible, though expressing in tangible form. Fact is that which we perceive with the physical senses; it is that which "appears to be." It may be either tangible or intangible, but to deny factual reality on the sense plane is to deny our reality as physical beings. Fact, as opposed to Truth, is subject to change and often falls short of the ideal. The Truth is that we are daughters and sons of God. The Lord—the law of our being—is indeed in His holy temple,[4] His wholeness etched with indelible clarity on our every cell.

"What right do you have to write about perfect patterns?" I asked myself as my son and I dined at a nearby restaurant. A handsome young man and his wife sat at the table next to ours. He was in a wheelchair and could not use his arms or legs. This was a fact; there was no denying the physical reality of it. Nevertheless, the Truth about him remains the same. The perfect pattern is there.

The young couple bowed their heads as he whispered a prayer. His wife cut his food and lovingly placed it in his mouth. He smiled and his face was filled with joy. He was whole and perfect! It was I who was in need of healing.

This event reminded me of a family I know whose baby daughter was born with a grossly deformed face and head. The parents were told by physicians that the child was so hopelessly retarded she would never be more than a vegetable. Through the faith of the family and the miracles of reconstructive surgery, she is today a normal little girl. The frontal lobes of her brain, which failed to appear on X ray, thus precipitating the diagnosis of retardation, were not missing at all. They were obscured by the skull malformation. I know of a man who, before the discovery of insulin, was cured of diabetes—still one of the so-called "incurable" diseases.[5]

Regardless of how hopeless a situation appears, it is for us as Truth students to know that the situation is only fact, not Truth, therefore subject to change. When we alter the way we think, we open ourselves to God's healing law and seeming miracles occur. Whatever the challenge, we must not give up. If anyone has ever been healed, then healing is possible for everyone. This does not mean that everyone will be healed, but the opportunity exists. Our job is to know that there are no incurable conditions and no situations that enough love and faith cannot heal.

Deep within the superconsciousness of us—

that part which is Spirit—there is engraved a pattern which God who created us knows us to be: perfect, undefiled, untouched by anything we have ever been. The Truth which frees is that we can, simply by changing our minds about ourselves and others, bring the facts of our lives into harmony with this perfect pattern.

Wholeness Is Your Heritage

Plato said, "In heaven is laid up a pattern which he who chooses may behold, and beholding, set his house in order."[6] The apostle Paul wrote, "If there is a physical body, there is also a spiritual body."[7] We might think of our body as composed of flesh and blood and bone and formed into a shape, which we call "human." Factually, this is correct. But the Truth is that each cell, each organ, is an expression in material form of an idea in the Mind of God—a *perfect* idea.

This is the "only begotten Son," the Christ man, out of which each of us evolves. Translated from the Mind of God and emblazoned on every cell of our body is the idea: *Wholeness is your heritage!*

All things are formed in the Mind of God through the process of involution, God's involvement in His creation. Through evolution these ideas unfold and take shape and form. Our individual body is the outpicturing of our concept of this God-idea. Whatever that concept might be, the Truth is that God's law of love for us is a perfect pattern. It is not only our privilege and duty to conform to this pattern, it is our inevitable destiny.

Consciousness Builds Our World

Spenser wrote:

> *For out of the soule the bodie forme doth take;*
> *For soule is forme and doth the bodie make.*[8]

Our mind is the builder of our world of "fact." Using the powerful tools of mind, we form our body and our world from substance—that "living energy out of which everything is made."[9]

This subtle building process takes place in the consciousness. Here every incident of life is recorded. From this composite picture of all of our thoughts and feelings, we, too, form a pattern—our individual concept of life. The Truth of us remains the perfect pattern that God knows us to be. This pattern, interpreted by our subjective mind, projects itself for good or ill into our world, as our world.

The Environmental Body

How do we see ourselves? Our jobs? Our homes? Our relationships with others? We see these as the outpicturing of our own thoughts and feelings. This is our environmental body, and it is just as real as our physical body. Both these bodies, in Truth, express perfect health, prosperity, and loving relationships. When they seemingly fall short of this ideal, we have the power to change what we see by changing the way we think and feel about it. This puts the responsibility for our happiness squarely on us. If we find ourselves in a situation not to our liking, we might well wish to return to our former way of thinking, where things happened *to* us, not through us. This cannot be done. We can never return to that "Edenic" innocence; nor should we want to, for we have grown to something greater. We know now the good news is that what we build, when not to our specifications, can be rebuilt in a more acceptable mode.

Thought and Feeling

There is an immutable law that what we hold in mind, with strong feeling or its equivalent, will inevitably come into being in our lives. Emotion should not be confused with feeling. Emotion, according to *The Revealing Word*, is "undisciplined or uncontrolled forces"[10] and of short duration. Feeling, however, has thought as its foundation; and though feelings and thoughts may be erroneous, they have power behind them, and their results are more enduring. Through a sudden burst of emotion, a person may be healed; but if there is no inner conviction to sustain that emotion, the healing is not likely to be permanent.

Jesus told us, "If two of you agree on earth about anything they ask, it will be done for them by my Father in heaven."[11] Symbolically, the two of whom Jesus spoke are our thinking and feeling natures. When these agree or reach a conviction that a thing is so, in Truth it is so, though on the material plane it may appear that time passes and certain events transpire before it comes into being. If our thinking and feeling natures were perfectly attended, we would manifest our good instantly, as Jesus did.

When we think one thing but feel another or feel one way and think another, we are in a mixed state of consciousness, and though we receive a little good, we get a little of what we do not want, as well. We are, as Jesus described, a "house divided."[12]

To merely think about something or wish for it is not enough. Nothing is truly ours until we reach a conviction that it belongs to us. After being chosen "Miss Universe, 1977," Janelle Commissiong of Trinidad-Tobago—the first black woman to receive that title—confided that she had a "gut feeling"[13] she would win. Coincidence? Perhaps, but I doubt it. We receive in the exact proportion for which we have the capacity to accept.

Sam, Sally, and Jane

Let me share with you the stories of three of my friends, each undergoing a similar appearance of disease. The first is the case of Sam Johnson who was in his mid-sixties at the time of his experience and a man with strong convictions of health. Sally's is the story of a "house divided." Though she understood spiritual healing intellectually, her feeling nature had not kept pace with her intellect. Jane's thinking and feeling natures were in complete accord—that there was no hope for recovery.

At the insistence of his wife, Sam entered the hospital for tests and (according to several specialists) extensive surgery due to a growth that was termed "almost certain to be malignant." From the beginning, Sam proved to be something less than the ideal patient. First of all, he refused to accept the doctors' verdict or to act as one suffering from so serious a problem. He would not wear the prescribed hospital gown or even the pajamas his wife brought for him. Nor would Sam stay in bed. Instead, dressed in a business suit, he roamed the halls, visiting each patient on his floor, telling jokes and discussing politics. The nurses, on discovering him walking about, scolded: "Mr. Johnson, what are you doing? You're suppose to be in bed!"

"Oh, I'm not *Sam* Johnson," Sam replied. "He's in his room. I'm his brother. Just dropped by for a little visit."

On election day Sam persuaded his doctor to check him out of the hospital for a short period so that he could vote. Sam never went back; though to placate his wife, he did visit his family physician to verify what he knew was true. The growth that had been clearly evident by manual examination and X ray had disappeared. Today Sam's perfect health continues and his doctors offer no convincing explanation.

Such bypassing of traditional treatment is not for everyone. Sam's affirmative attitude was not developed overnight. Nor was he attempting to test God's healing law. Sam had been a practitioner of the principles of positive living all of his life. He saw good in every person and every situation. He refused to entertain negative thoughts. He *knew* with a conviction that transcended mere belief or emotion that he was a perfect child of God, and he made it his business to act that way.

My friend Sally also discovered a suspicious growth. She prayed and received the assurance that if she would heal her fear, the disharmonious condition would correct itself. She believed this, but the habitual thinking of a lifetime was more than she was able to quickly overcome. Sally was a Truth student, but her feeling nature had not yet assimilated all that her intellect hungrily grasped. Being a sensible person, she realized that since the condition did not appear to be improving, it was time to seek God's help through another agency of faith—the physician. The growth was successfully removed by surgery.

Sally's challenge was healed at the level in which her thinking and feeling natures could agree—not so desirable a method as Sam's, but effective nonetheless.

Less happy an outcome was Jane's. Though she outwardly accepted the teachings of Truth, she could not conceive of overcoming such a disease as that diagnosed by her doctors. She wanted to believe she could be healed, but the evidence of her senses told her otherwise. An outline of treatment was proposed, but Jane was too ill to begin. Each day her condition deteriorated and within six weeks she was dead. According to her physicians, her death was not due to the effects of the illness, but to simply giving up.

These people represent three levels of the mind's ability to heal the body. Each received the exact fruit of his or her thinking and feeling natures.

Decide and Desire

We have within our consciousness two marvelous powers that inevitably bring to us whatever we choose: the power of decision and the power of desire. Decision is the activity of the thinking nature. When we decide what we want, we take the first step toward creating a productive pattern for our life. If we have a clear picture of what we want, we are on our way to achieving it. If we have only a vague notion of what we want, this is precisely what we receive. If we do not decide, the world will decide for us.

The word *decide* comes from the Latin *decidere*,

which means "to cut off from."[14] As an incision cleanly cuts its surgical mark, when we reach a "decision" we cut, with the same mental precision, that which we want from that which we do not want.

Desire is the activity of the feeling nature. It has been said that desire for anything is the beginning of the desired thing becoming yours. H. Emilie Cady in *Lessons in Truth* writes, "The thing you desire is not only for you but has already been started toward you out of the heart of God; it is the first approach . . . striking you that makes you desire it or even think of it at all."[15] When we put the full force of our feelings behind our longing for the perfect pattern, it becomes a drawing power, acting as a magnet whose only goal is to bring to us that which we have chosen.

To expand the consciousness, we must convince the subjective mind that what we have decided upon and desire is *already* ours, that we are the person we want to be, and that our world is a loving and joyful place. Jesus said: "Do you not say, 'There are yet four months, then comes the harvest'? I tell you, lift up your eyes, and see how the fields are already white for harvest."[16]

Thought, Word, Action

Only we human beings have at our disposal three marvelous powers to make our life a heaven or a hell: the powers of thought, word, and action. As children of God, our potential is limitless. By expanding our consciousness, there is nothing we cannot do or be. Our only limitation is that which we place on ourselves.

We are threefold beings—Spirit, soul, and body—and in this three-dimensional world three steps—thought, word, and action—are necessary to demonstrate our good. When we control these activities within ourselves, there is nothing we cannot accomplish. At the end of this chapter and the following eleven chapters, you will find some "tri-level" suggestions for expanding your attunement to God's laws of love.

———————◀○▶———————

Pattern Practices

1. Develop your faith. Faith is the fruit of the marriage of the thinking and feeling natures.

Faith is the power that perceives and forms out of substance that which we desire. Have faith that there is in Truth a perfect pattern for your body—your physical body and the body of your affairs. It exists. It is real—more real than the so-called world of form in which we live. "Be still, and know."[17] Practice preventive meditation.

2. Know that the will of God is good. You have a right to your good. There is an ancient maxim that states, "As above, so below." If a thing is good on Earth, it is surely a good idea in the Mind of God. Never accept the belief that misfortune is the will of God, though good can rise out of any situation. God's will for His children is always the abundant life.

3. Avoid the infiltration of negatives into your consciousness. Few persons today believe that we can be possessed by evil spirits; yet most of us are to some degree influenced by the evil spirit of negative newspaper headlines, stock averages, medical statistics, other people's opinions, even the weather. Cast out these demons! Exorcize them before they take permanent residence in your temple.

4. Watch your words. The subjective mind takes all statements literally. Avoid such phrases as: *I'm sorry about. . . . I hate to think that. . . . I'm afraid it will. . . . She makes me sick! . . . He's breaking my heart. . . . I'm so mad I could die!*

   Also avoid attaching unwanted characteristics to yourself or others: *I'm a worrier. She's a pest. He's accident-prone.* Even worse is the naming of yourself or another as the possessor of certain diseases. Never say, "I am a _____," and then play the game of Name That Malady. This is not your identity! You may experience a particular condition, but the condition is not who you are! Never refer to a condition as "my _____," unless you want it as a permanent boarder.

5. Deny and overcome past beliefs in limitation. Families, cultures, and religious groups perpetuate these prejudices, with no one daring to call their bluff and deny their validity. Truly, the sins (failures to achieve the goal) of the fathers are visited upon the children for generations.[18] But they need not be!

6. Affirm the Truth. You are a good and wor-

thy human being. This is the Truth about you. Feel good about yourself. Tell your body—physical and environmental—that it is good. Then watch it respond! Your body is your friend. Praise it, for praise strengthens and increases that which it is lavished upon. Say aloud: "You are a good body. I love and appreciate you!"

7. Act as if you are the person you want to be. Feel as you would feel if you were now this person. Act as if you have achieved the goal that you desire. Feel as you would feel if it were now in your possession. Visualize your desire as an accomplished fact. Remember that like attracts like. We become like that which we contemplate. As comedian Flip Wilson so aptly puts it, "What you see is what you get!" Now give thanks that you have received your good.

8. Take appropriate action in the outer world. Carry through on your ideas. Many Truth students stop before reaching this step. It is fun to visualize. It is interesting to "deny and affirm." But action takes effort and is not always so pleasant. A goal, however, can never

be achieved through mind-power alone. Action is an essential ingredient for accomplishment on this plane of existence. To desire to be healed but abuse the laws of good health is foolishness. To affirm prosperity but then refuse employment is counterproductive. While a slave, educator Frederick Douglass prayed for freedom. Later he admitted that his prayers were not answered until they reached his heels and he ran away from his former life.

9. Persist. Persistence is faith in action. The story is told that after 50,000 experiments on the storage battery, Thomas Edison was asked if he had achieved any success. "Why, of course!" Mr. Edison replied. "I know 50,000 ways that don't work!" How can we give up after a few paltry attempts to achieve our goal? Who knows? That next attempt may be the one that brings our heart's desire.

Chapter 2

Abundance

*"Fear not, little flock, for it is your
Father's good pleasure to give . . ."*[1]

The teacher stood before the people who had
gathered to hear his words and be healed of their
infirmities. As the day wore on, his closest students reminded him that it was growing late and
the people must be sent on their way to obtain
food. The teacher replied that the people need
not leave, that they—his disciples—should provide the food. It was surely with heavy hearts that
these twelve gazed at that vast sea of hungry faces.
Sadly, they told their master that there were only
five loaves and two fish, far from enough food for
so many. "Bring them here to me," the teacher

told them; then taking the food, he looked up and blessed and broke it. Then he gave it to his disciples who distributed it among the crowd. Everyone ate and was satisfied, and there were twelve baskets left over. [2]

This is Jesus' master prosperity lesson. The importance of this particular demonstration of abundance is exemplified by the fact that it is one of the few stories told in each of the four Gospels.[3] By certain definite and distinct steps, Jesus was able to provide more than enough food to feed 5000 men (plus, we are told, women and children).

The word *prosperity* comes from the Latin *prosperitas*, which means an "advance or gain in anything good or desirable."[4] Prosperity includes not only wealth (though sufficient money to meet our needs is essential to true prosperity) but health, happiness, loving relationships, and all the good things of life. Real prosperity benefits not only the one receiving, but all humankind as well.

God's law is the abundance of all good and desirable things. God loves to give. It is His nature to give. It is His joy to give. We see proof of God's generosity in all nature. The trees are not clothed scantily. An ear of corn is not barely covered, but covered with an abundance of grain. We visualize a snowfall and know that no two flakes are ever alike. In our own body, should injury occur, millions of cells rush to our assistance to repair whatever the need might be. Nature is overly generous!

Consider the musical composer. Though he creates the most beautiful symphony, it is but odd squiggles on a piece of paper until the musicians take up their instruments and play. God is the Master Composer. We are God's musicians. God has given us His most beautiful score and limitless access to the instruments of abundance. Should we not perform as perfectly as possible? Like the composer whose goal is fulfilled through the musicians playing in harmony, God enjoys, experiences, and loves through our abundant living. How can we refuse God's bountiful gifts, thereby denying God His rightful expression on this earthly plane?

Some refuse the riches of life because they do not know how to "play" the marvelous instruments of abundance. But they need not, for

Jesus teaches that if we follow his guidance with these "Seven Rs to Receptivity," we shall all have abundant life.

Step #1: Relaxation

When we read the story of the feeding of the 5000, we find nothing specifically stating that Jesus made a conscious effort to relax. From his own statements, however, a constant state of relaxation is implied: "Come to me, all who labor and are heavy laden, and I will give you rest."[5] "Peace I leave with you; my peace I give to you."[6] "Come away by yourselves to a lonely place, and rest a while."[7] It is all but impossible to imagine an "uptight" Jesus.

The Revealing Word defines *relaxation* as "a letting go of tenseness in mind and body. Abatement of strain. Loosening the tight mental grip we have on ourselves in order that the healing Christ life may flow freely through our being."[8]

Books have been written, lectures offered, and instructions given teaching the techniques of physical relaxation. Though proper nutrition, adequate rest, and exercise are essential to our well-being, it would appear that our frantic efforts to relax the physical body are like putting the cart before the horse.

The body is an agreeable machine. It follows the instructions of the mind without question. When we feel as though our body is wound up like a steel band, unless there is a definite physical cause, this tenseness does not originate with the body, but with our thoughts. When the mind relaxes, the body relaxes as well.

But how do we accomplish this stilling of the mind and body? A regular time and place to meet with God are essential. Our thoughts are amenable to habit and, just as they pick up undesirable habits, they as quickly recognize the sanctity of a certain time and place set aside for meeting with the Father. So to begin, position yourself comfortably. Relax and bless each part of your body. Think of your mind as a tunnel at the end of which is a fertile field where you plant the seed of your desire. Then gently filter out thoughts that interfere with your concentration, for extraneous thoughts clutter the tunnel and become an obstacle to reaching the goal.

Gently is the key word to putting away these

thoughts. To struggle is to create a monster that brings more and stronger disruptive thoughts. Our first attempts at this type of mental relaxation may not be total successes. This should not disturb us, for with practice and patience we will succeed. Remember that our thoughts are accustomed to having their way, to being allowed to barge into the privacy of our consciousness whenever they choose. Like unruly children, they must be disciplined to refrain from such inappropriate intrusions. But gently . . .

Step #2: Recognition

The recognition of a need is our next step toward the demonstration of our goal. When the disciples were faced with feeding 5000 persons, the need was specific and obvious: food.

Our needs may not be so easily defined. Too often we fail to achieve our desires simply because we are not sure what they might be. We may be experiencing a vague longing, a sense of discontent, yet feel uncertain as to what we need to satisfy these stirrings. To receive, we must first know precisely what it is that we want. We must define it and dedicate ourselves to it. If we want roses, we do not plant onion bulbs. We must be specific. The law is exacting. God knows how to bring about whatever we desire. But do we know what we really want?

Some may ask: "Do I have the right to ask for 'things'? Isn't that selfish?" Philanthropist Andrew Carnegie was visited by a socialist who berated him regarding the inequity of one man's possessing so much money. Carnegie asked his secretary for a statement of his holdings; then from the almanac he looked up the figures on world population. He figured for a few moments, then reached into his pocket and handed the man 16 cents. "Take it," he told him. "This is your share of my wealth."

It has been said that if all the money in the world were pooled, then evenly distributed, within six months the money would be back with its original holder.

We are Spirit, soul, and body. Spirit, in its essence, is formless. It can only express in this world through form. As form, it is no less spiritual. We live in a world of constantly changing forms. Either these forms control us or we control them. When we align our thoughts with that which is unchanging, spiritual substance automatically expresses in our life as health, prosperity, friendships. It also appears in such tangible ways as houses, jobs, and money. Charles Fillmore wrote, "Translate material desires into their spiritual correspondents and then declare that in Truth and in Spirit you receive that which you desire, and then you will have it materially as well as spiritually."[9]

Have you recognized your goal? Is there a desire in your heart yearning to be fulfilled? Evidence proves beyond the slightest doubt that anything we truly desire can be achieved. I have seen this come about in situations that appeared hopeless. I have experienced it in my own life.

But the key word is *truly*. If your desire is irrational, such as would be the case if a man's greatest goal in life were to become Miss America, you might want to reassess your goals. As Charles Fillmore advised, when you translate material desires into their spiritual equivalent, you will find that it is self-expression and love which you "truly" desire.

We have been conditioned by outer circumstances to believe that some things are impossible, or at least unlikely to achieve. As a result, we must first change our belief before our demonstration can come about. God is able to provide for 5000 as easily as for five. However, this is hard for us to believe.

Ring Lardner suggested: "A good many young writers make the mistake of enclosing a stamped, self-addressed envelope, big enough for the manuscript to come back in. This is too much of a temptation to the editor."[10] He may have been right. We must believe in our goals.

A total commitment is essential. Achievement requires a singleness of purpose. There can be no mental or physical reservations. With every doubt, we chip away a portion of our creation. If our desire is good for us and beneficial—or at least harmless—to everyone else, then we should love it enough to work for it wholeheartedly.

Just as we cannot achieve a goal that someone else has set for us, neither can we interfere with the goals of others. The goal we recognize must be what *we* want, not what someone else wants for us nor what we think we ought to want. We can and should assist others through prayer, encouragement, and helpful actions when requested to do so, but the desire must be the individual's own.

Jesus took the recognition of need to its ultimate. He recognized God as the Fulfiller of all needs, the Source of all supply—"He looked up to heaven."[11] We, too, should recognize this same Truth. We need not be concerned as to the channel through which our good will come. There are infinite channels and the Father knows each of them. God's promise is that even if we lose one of our channels of supply, we can be sure that another will appear—expressing the exact equivalent of our consciousness of abundance.

Step #3: Realization

Realization, the marriage between the thinking (masculine) and feeling (feminine) natures, is the third step toward demonstrating our desires. To bring this about, we work with these faculties until our belief becomes a conviction that what we desire is *now* ours.

We are told that Jesus "broke and gave the loaves to the disciples." The breaking of bread, according to *The Revealing Word*, refers to the "stirring into action . . . of the inner substance of Spirit. . . ."[12] Fish "represent ideas of multiplication . . . ideas in which there is great possibility of increase; Jesus used these ideas to represent the inexhaustible, everywhere present abundance."[13]

There were two fish, representing the thinking power given man to build up or dissolve by his word. "Let what you say be simply 'Yes' or 'No'," Jesus advised.[14] To convince the thinking nature, we affirm that we have all that we desire now. We deny any appearance to the contrary.

There were five loaves of bread. Metaphysically, the number *five* represents the physical senses. It is through the senses that we convince our feeling nature that what we have conceived is, in fact, ours. We perceive that we are already in possession of our good: we see it, we hear the sound of it, we smell its scent, we savor its flavor, we feel its touch. And most important, we feel as we would feel if it were ours now.

Thus when marriage takes place in consciousness between the thinking and feeling natures, realization occurs, and the demonstration is complete, even though not yet manifest in the outer world.

Step #4: Rejoicing

In the story of Jesus' great demonstration we are told that he "blessed . . . the loaves." He gave thanks in advance. His faith was so great that even though his outer vision perceived only two fish and five loaves, his insight told him that already the demonstration was complete. Jesus often practiced this attitude of giving thanks in advance. One notable occasion was at the death of his friend Lazarus. Though Lazarus had been in his tomb for four days, Jesus prayed, saying, "Father, I thank thee that thou hast heard me." Then he commanded, "Lazarus, come out." Lazarus did, still bound in his burial cloths, but vibrant with life.[15]

Giving thanks in advance should not be so difficult a concept, for doing so is a part of our daily experience. If we telephone a department store to order an item and are told that it will arrive in three days if our credit is good, we thank the salesperson, confident that our order will be filled. We do not wait until the item arrives, then call the store to say, "Thank you." We can be certain that our credit is good with the Father and our order is filled, whatever we ask.

The story is told of a father who gave his young son a dime and a quarter when he went to his Sunday school class. "Put whichever you decide into the collection," the father said, curious as to which the boy would choose. After church he asked his son which coin he gave. "Well," the boy replied, "I remember the minister saying that 'the Lord loveth a cheerful giver,' so I figured I'd be a lot more cheerful if I gave the dime and kept the quarter!" There is truth in the boy's logic. Giving is the other side of receiving, a way of saying, "Thank you." But if not done with joy, it is worthless.

Thousands of years ago, the Hebrew people discovered the benefits derived from giving a tenth of all they had to Jehovah. Others who have tried tithing have discovered that even though we do not give for the purpose of receiving, receiving is the natural result. "Bring the full tithes into the storehouse . . . and thereby put me to the test, says the Lord of hosts, if I will not open the windows of heaven for you and pour down for you an overflowing blessing."[16]

Quite a challenge! Are we up to it?

Step #5: Response

Had Jesus stopped after blessing the loaves, his disciples would have been left holding the bread. Instead, he gave it to them and they distributed it among the people. They took action.

When James A. Garfield was president of Hiram College, a father brought his son to be enrolled. He insisted that his son was so bright that it would be a waste of time for him to take the full course. "Can't you arrange a shorter term for him?" the father asked.

"Certainly," Mr. Garfield responded. "He can take a shorter course. It all depends on what he wants to make of himself. When God wants an oak, He spends a hundred years. But He can make a squash in only two months."

It is the natural order that we work to bring into being those things which we want. By giving up too soon, we may stop just short of success. Once we have determined what we truly desire, we must put all of our effort into achieving this goal. To hold back for whatever reason is an admission of our lack of faith. When tempted to quit, we might remember the oak and the squash. A squash is good for one meal, but an oak provides shade and beauty and food for generations.

Step #6: Release

For many action-oriented individuals, the act of release can be the most difficult of all. It is essential, however, and we must trust our intuitive judgment to know when the time is right. Then, as Paul so wisely put it, "having done all, to stand."[17]

Jesus described it this way:

> "The kingdom of God is as if a man should scatter seed upon the ground, and should sleep and rise night and day, and the seed should sprout and grow, he knows not how. The earth produces of itself, first the blade, then the ear, then the full grain in the ear." [18]

When we plant a seed, we know that within

that seed is all the knowledge needed to produce after its kind. If we go out each day and dig it up to see how it is doing, it will die. So it is with the seed planted in consciousness. Randomly discussing our goals or thinking about them excessively or with negativity can have the same disastrous effect as uprooting the tender young sprout.

Though it may appear that little is taking place during this spiritual Sabbath, great activity is going on in secret. "Not by might, nor by power, but by my Spirit, says the Lord of hosts."[19]

Step #7: Receiving

The time inevitably comes when that which we have planted comes to fruition. Reaping, however, is not always so easy as it seems. All of us know people who are generous givers, but poor receivers. When Jesus multiplied the loaves and fish, the people had a choice. He provided the food, and the disciples brought it to them; but the people had to take it, put it in their mouths, chew, and swallow it themselves. They had the freedom to refuse to receive.

Mark

"I guess I believe in Emerson's law of compensation," my young friend Mark told me dejectedly.

"Oh?" I replied. "And what is that?"

"Well," Mark began, "it's like this. If you have a certain amount of good things happen, then you will have an equal amount of things that aren't so good, just to balance it out." Earlier in the year Mark, an honor student, had won several awards, played the lead in the school play, been elected president of a prestigious youth organization, and had several young ladies competing for his attentions. In the week prior to our talk, however, Mark had received a "D" on one of his report cards, lost the lead in the spring musical, and failed to be elected junior class president. To make matters worse, that very day he had walked off and left his band uniform in the school yard. Mark had been "grounded" until further notice by his bewildered parents.

"Do you really think it's 'compensation'?" I asked, ignoring Mark's misinterpretation of Emerson's essay. "It sounds a little like you may have placed limitations on the number of 'good things' that can happen."

I had his attention. "What do you mean?" he asked.

I was sure that Mark had been sufficiently lectured on the consequences of carelessness, poor study habits, and improper priorities. Since he considered himself somewhat the philosopher, I decided to try a different approach. "If you think of yourself as a second-rate person and something comes along that puts you in the position of being a first-rate person, you may accept it and even think it's great, but so long as you carry an image of yourself as second-rate, you'll find some way to lose in order to preserve that image. Right?"

"Hmmm . . ." Mark murmured thoughtfully.

"But you're not a number," I continued. "You're a person, and it's not necessary to put limitations on yourself."

I do not maintain that the profundity of my message changed Mark's life, though his challenges appear to have subsided. I wonder, however, how much good each of us fails to receive as a result of our own self-imposed limitations.

How High Is Your "RQ"?

There was a time when tremendous importance was placed on the measurement of a person's intelligence by certain IQ (intelligence quotient) tests. Once the IQ score was indelibly inscribed on one's records, that person was categorized for life. These scores were believed an infallible and unalterable determinator of the individual's capabilities and potentialities. They became science's fortune-teller.

Though IQ tests are still helpful guidelines, they are no longer so rigidly adhered to. It is known that factors other than an individual's inherent intelligence influence performance on these tests. It is also recognized that other elements influence our performance in life—persistence, the desire to achieve, the encouragement we receive from parents and others. It has also been found that by learning how to take these tests, individuals can actually raise their IQ scores. That was a shocking concept a few years ago!

In much the same way we can learn how to raise our receptivity quotient, our RQ. In the sixties there was a show on television called *The*

Prisoner. Much to his despair, the leading character was assigned the title, Number Six. He kept insisting: "I am a man. I am not a number." Though we may not realize it, each of us is in much that same position. We should be as adamant as "the prisoner" in our insistence that we are not a number, but an idea of unlimited potential in the Mind of God—a human being!

a = RQ

The capital letter *A* stands for God's universal abundance, everywhere present and unlimited, waiting to be called into being and formed by man. The little letter *a* is our portion of this abundance. It is an equation. Our abundance equals our receptivity quotient. Knowing this, our prayer does not become one of attempting to influence God's givingness. Our prayer must be to expand our own receptivity.

———————◄○►———————

Receptivity Raisers

1. RELAX your body and mind. RECOG-
   NIZE your need and the Source who will
   supply the fulfillment of that need. REAL-
   IZE that your desire is fulfilled—now.
2. REJOICE. Give thanks aloud that you have
   received your good. Become aware of the
   great abundance you already possess. Revel
   in the joy of it. Joy is a wonderful thanks-
   giver! Affirm that all you need is yours, then
   deny all appearance of limitation.
3. RESPOND. Take positive action to bring
   your good to you. Use is the rule. That
   which is productively used is always replaced with more than enough.
4. RELEASE your efforts. Do not stir the cake
   while it bakes in the oven. Your desire
   knows how to become without your interference.
5. Be willing to RECEIVE. When your Father
   offers a gift, do not insult Him by saying,
   "No." A story is told of a man who dreamed
   that he died. As St. Peter gave him a tour of
   heaven, they entered a building containing

the most wonderful things he had ever seen. "What are these things?" the man asked.

"This is the celestial storage room," St. Peter told him, "and these are the answered prayers that people refused to claim." Be a gracious receiver. Remember that we demonstrate the exact equivalent of our ability to receive.

Chapter 3

Compensation

"I will restore to you the years which the swarming locust has eaten."[1]

Ralph Waldo Emerson in his essay, "Compensation," wrote:

> Men suffer all their life long under the foolish superstition that they can be cheated. But it is as impossible for a man to be cheated by anyone but himself, as for a thing to be and not to be, at the same time. There is a third silent partner to all our bargains. The nature and soul of things takes on itself the guaranty of the

fulfillment of every contract, so that honest service cannot come to loss. If you serve an ungrateful master, serve him the more. Put God in your debt. Every stroke shall be repaid. The longer the payment is withholden, the better for you; for compound interest on compound interest is the rate and usage of this exchequer.[2]

One of the hardest lessons to be learned is that we do not receive in the exact manner and time that *we* choose. The law of compensation is immutable, returning to us far more than we could hope to receive were we allowed to set our own limits. But it must work in its own way and its own time. Three of my friends found this a challenging lesson.

Mary, Paul, and Eleanor

"I'm not going to do one more thing for that organization," Mary told me. A special service award she had expected to receive was presented to another. "I work my fingers to the bone, but do I get any appreciation? No! At least ten people told me how badly they thought I'd been treated!"

Paul's lament was similar. "I worked there twenty years. Stayed overtime whenever they asked, and boy, did they ask! Even worked weekends and holidays! I really thought they appreciated me. Then when a supervisory position opens, what happens? They hire someone from outside! Hmphhhh!" he snorted. "Everybody says it's not fair!" Eleanor's efforts were a little closer to home—her own. "I'm simply through with all this!" she loudly proclaimed as she placed the finishing touches on a dress for her daughter. "I'll never cook another meal, iron another shirt, or make a bed for them! Do they spend any time with me or care how I feel? Do they show any gratitude? A bunch of ingrates, that's what they are!" Eleanor was not referring to boarders or dependent offspring, but to her three adult "children" who made their home with her and her husband.

Each of my friends made a common error in judgment. They expected a reward equal to service rendered, from the source to which it had been rendered and at a time specified by themselves.

When that reward was not forthcoming, they became angry and frustrated.

These two truths are often forgotten: First, there is no service, lovingly and willingly rendered, that ever goes without reward. "Cast your bread upon the waters, for you will find it after many days."[3] Second, the reward seldom comes from the source to which service was given.

The Revealing Word describes *compensation* as "the order under which one receives just remuneration. The law of compensation is universal and not subject to personal demands. If the mind is turned toward man as one's recompense, it is turned away from divine law."[4]

These three friends had given unstintingly of themselves—for the purpose of being rewarded. Like the hypocrites described by Jesus as practicing their piety to be seen by men,[5] they, too, had been unequivocally rewarded. Paul and Mary were bathed in the sympathy of associates. Visible martyrdom was Eleanor's natural return. Giving of one's self is much like giving of one's financial resources. Receiving is the natural consequence; but if we give only to receive, then we are rewarded by man and that reward is notoriously unfulfilling.

If we feel we are not receiving our just dues, we might ask, "Is my giving self-oriented or love-oriented?" Eleanor had far too long "served" her children. It is no wonder they were ungrateful. The greatest service she could have given would have been to allow them the freedom to stand on their own feet. She had overdone herself in doing for them—for herself. In this same way, Mary and Paul had turned toward the world for their recompense, thus away from divine law.

I like Emerson's idea of having a "third silent partner" to all my bargains and "putting God in my debt." I once met a man who understood this thoroughly.

My Angel Unaware

Out of necessity I was driving through what could most generously be described as a "questionable" neighborhood. Suddenly, the lights on the dashboard flashed red, buzzers sounded, and smoke began pouring from beneath the hood of my car. There were no service stations available to make repairs, no businesses or houses where I felt I could safely ask to use a telephone. There seemed nothing to do but pull over to the side of the road and wait for a police car to come by.

Now I know that each of us has been given talents, but with no damage to my self-esteem I long ago recognized and accepted the fact that mechanical aptitude was not mine. Generally, this does not concern me; but at that moment, it seemed the greatest of spiritual gifts.

Almost immediately a pickup truck pulled up behind me and a man who looked as if he belonged in the neighborhood emerged from it. Being in no bargaining position, I whispered a prayer and rolled my window down an inch or so.

"Having trouble?" he asked, smiling.

I rolled the window down a bit more. It was summer and the temperature was nearing a hundred. "My car seems to be overheated. Would you telephone my husband for me?" I offered him a scrap of paper on which I had hastily scrawled Frank's business number.

Ignoring my request, he went to the front of the car, threw open the hood, and peered intently inside. "Here's your trouble," he called out. Cautiously, I stepped from the car. He pointed to a particular part. "This is busted. It's gotta be replaced. You'll tear up the car if you drive it."

I looked about more closely. There were private clubs, liquor stores, and massage parlors, but nothing that looked as if it might carry automotive parts.

"There's a repair shop about a mile from here," he went on. "They oughta have it. I'll take you there and if they have the part, I can fix your car in short order."

"Um . . . " I murmured, glancing nervously in the direction of his truck. Friend or foe . . . ? Dear God, what do I do?

No, I firmly decided. I would not get in a vehicle and drive away with a total stranger. This was not lack of faith. It was merely good judgment. I would thank him politely, then wait for the rest of the day, if need be, till Frank came home from work and missed me or a police car came by. Surely, a police car would be by soon . . .

He shook his head as he scanned our surroundings. "You'd better stay with the car. This ain't the best part of town, you know. I know it's hot, but get in and keep those doors locked till I get back. I won't be long."

Heaving a sigh of relief, I opened my bill-fold. Only money was now at stake. "How much will the part cost?" I ventured.

"About ten dollars."

Little enough, I noted, and offered the bill. He waved it away. "Pay me when I get back."

He returned shortly with the necessary equipment, at a cost of less than ten dollars, then in a few minutes informed me that the car was "as good as new."

"How much do I owe you?" I asked, barely believing my good fortune. The car was humming contentedly and no flashing lights or buzzers warned of trouble.

"You don't owe me anything."

"But I *want* to give you something for your trouble."

"Someday you'll meet someone who needs help and when you do, you'll help. That's the way you'll repay me."

"But what's your name?" I persisted. "I don't know what I'd have done without you. And my husband will want to thank you, too, for all the work you've done."

He merely smiled.

For several blocks I followed his truck to get the license number in order to find out who he was. Cars kept getting between us, then finally I lost sight of him completely. Later that afternoon when Frank examined the car, he was amazed at the professional job that had been done in finding the problem and correcting it.

For some time I expected a dramatic incident when I would know that this was my moment to repay his kindness. It never came. Small things occurred, things that took my time and tried my patience, but nothing that seemed equal to that which I had received. I finally realized that my friend had left me with a debt which will likely be repaid in installments for the rest of my life.

Wherever he is, I bless him and know that he is collecting interest on his investments. I had personally been given the scriptural lesson: "Do not neglect to show hospitality to strangers, for by doing that some have entertained angels without knowing it."[6]

The Birth of Seth

Compensation is one of the first laws taught in the Bible. In the book of Genesis, we read that Adam and Eve had two sons. The older, Cain, killed his brother Abel.[7] Metaphysically, offspring represent thoughts evolving from an original or parent idea. The "name" given to anything defines its nature. In Hebrew, the name *Abel* means "breath,"[8] indicating the mental realm, a step forward in the development of physical man. *Cain*, however, means "possession, acquisition."[9] He was a tiller of the soil, a man of the earth. In this allegory, we find the mental in conflict with the physical, and as so often happens, the acquisitive and unillumined physical nature—that part which believes it can take what it wants by force—appears to be the victor. "The spirit indeed is willing, but the flesh is weak."[10]

The idea behind this allegory is that there is a balancing power in nature and that no force can keep from us that which is ours by right of consciousness. Abel was conceived and brought forth out of the union of the thinking (Adam) and the feeling (Eve) natures. He belonged to this union by right of consciousness. Therefore, another son was born to Adam and Eve, who "called his name Seth, for she said, 'God has appointed for me another child instead of Abel, for Cain slew him.'" [11] Two of the Hebrew meanings for the name *Seth* are "substituted" and "compensation."[12] The "Abel" idea was legitimate and by law had to be compensated.

On the other hand, we can never possess that which is not ours by right of consciousness. To our human vision it might appear that success is achieved dishonestly, that the corrupt prosper, and the devious receive the spoils. The will is a powerful tool, and it may seem to prevail for a time. But it is only a tool, and we can be sure that one can only hold that which is taken by the force of will so long as will continues to be exerted. Once the guard is let down, as it inevitably will be, that which was taken dishonestly is lost. Just as Cain became a fugitive and a wanderer[13] as a result of attempting to destroy the higher impulses symbolized by his brother, every erroneous act has inherent within it its own consequence. "For truly,

I say to you, till heaven and earth pass away, not an iota, not a dot, will pass from the law until all is accomplished."[14]

How Much Does God Compensate?

Is it an equation? we might wonder. Is our compensation equal to our loss? Paul said, "Do not be deceived; God is not mocked, for whatever a man sows, that he will also reap."[15] Jesus presented a loftier view. "Give, and it will be given to you; good measure, pressed down, shaken together, running over, will be put into your lap."[16]

We never suffer the appearance of loss without the law of universal balance stepping in and setting straight our equilibrium. The greater the challenge, the greater the compensation. The only stipulation is that we use what we have.

Some of H. G. Wells' greatest books were written as he recuperated from a serious illness. French Impressionist painter Renoir experienced such pain from arthritis that, even though he was unable to use his arms, he continued to paint with brushes strapped to his hands. Journalist Joseph Pulitzer was blind, as was writer James Thurber.

Tchaikovsky suffered chronic depression, yet he gave to the world music unsurpassed in beauty and depth of feeling. Artist Toulouse-Lautrec was crippled as well as deformed. The Stoic philosopher Epictetus was not only lame, but a slave as well. Scientist Charles Steinmetz was a hunchback. Both Julius Caesar and Alexander the Great, renowned military leaders, underwent the seizure of epilepsy, as did painter Vincent van Gogh. English poet Lord Byron had a crippled leg. Homer, author of *The Iliad* and *The Odyssey*, was blind, as was the poet Milton. Rough Rider and United States President Theodore Roosevelt was a sickly, nervous child with poor eyesight, who was told that he must live a sheltered and sedate life. Beethoven, though deaf, composed and directed music heard only in his mind. Franklin D. Roosevelt, four-times-elected President of the United States, was unable to walk or even to stand. Athenian orator Demosthenes overcame stuttering by speaking with pebbles in his mouth over the noise of the ocean's roar. Helen Keller, though blind and deaf since early childhood and with a speech impediment, inspired the world by her accomplishments as an author and educator.

Many have suspected that their achievements came not in *spite* of their challenges, but as a result of them. It was suggested to Thomas A. Edison by a specialist in ear disease that his hearing might be restored. Edison flatly refused his offer of treatment. "What I'm afraid of," he responded, "is that you might be successful. To be deaf allows me to concentrate. Just think of all the stuff I don't have to listen to!"

Actress Sarah Bernhardt lost a leg, but did not lose her sense of humor. Shortly after the amputation, she received a request from the manager of the Pan-American Exposition at San Francisco, offering $100,000 for permission to display her leg. Immediately, she cabled back, "Which leg?" Her acting career continued uninterrupted for many years.

Louis Braille, who developed the braille system of printing for the blind, was blind himself from the age of three.

The law of compensation does not apply exclusively to physical disharmonies. A number of best-sellers were written while their authors were imprisoned. John Bunyan wrote the largest portion of *Pilgrim's Progress* while incarcerated. Miguel de Cervantes, who had only one arm, began *Don Quixote* while in prison. Daniel Defoe wrote *Hymns to the Pillory* from a jail cell. Others who wrote from prisons are Jawaharlal Nehru while serving a ten-year sentence and Marco Polo who dictated *The Travels of Marco Polo* to a fellow prisoner. O. Henry, while serving a five-year sentence, wrote some of his best short stories. Sir Walter Raleigh in the Tower of London wrote his *History of the World*. Oscar Wilde, while serving a sentence in Reading Jail, convicted on charges of homosexuality, wrote, among other things, *Ballad of Reading Gaol*.

The seeming loss of financial security has often resulted in greater gain for those who were receptive to the opportunity offered. Nathaniel Hawthorne lost his job and, feeling desperate and dejected, returned home to tell his wife of their misfortune. "Good!" was her unexpected response. "Now you'll have time to work on your book." *The Scarlet Letter* was written during this period.

Other "handicaps" have turned into victories. As a first lieutenant in the Air Force, Daniel James risked being court-martialed in order to fight segregation. During his thirty-four-year military career, he was a staunch defender of equal rights. Today the photograph of "Chappie" James, the nation's first black four-star general, hangs in the Pentagon and on it are inscribed his words: "I love America and as she has weaknesses or ills, I'll hold her hand."[17]

We may have experienced the loss of someone dear to us. As human beings, we find it difficult to part with those we love, whatever the cause. We question how such a loss can ever be compensated. After the death of my father, my mother—a loving and compassionate person—refused to visit anyone in the hospital where he had been. For more than four years she kept her vow, insisting that the memories were too painful. Then early one morning my daughter was born—her first grandchild—and she was there in that same hospital to greet her compensation. Emerson explained it this way: "We cannot let our angels go. We do not see that they go out that archangels may come in."[18]

One of the greatest examples of overcoming obstacles is found in the New Testament. The apostle Paul speaks of a "thorn . . . in the flesh."[19] It is indeed to his credit that no one knows just what this "thorn" might have been. What we do know, however, is that it in no way hindered him in his dedication to the task of spreading the good news of Christianity.

How much does God compensate? There is no limit. The only limitation is that which we place upon ourselves through our refusal to use that which we have and our inability to accept that which the Father lovingly offers to us.

The Remnant

Running through the Old Testament from its beginning is the idea of the "remnant." From a literal point of view, this "remnant" referred to those Jews, regardless of how small in number, who remained faithful in their worship and followed Jehovah. No matter how hopeless things appeared, there was always the promise that a "remnant" would be preserved.

The prophet Joel lived in Jerusalem after that remnant of faithful Jews returned to Judah following the Babylonian exile. At that time the land had been ravaged by swarms of locusts, leaving the crops in waste. The destruction was so devastating that no one could recall a disaster equal to it.

Joel was not the compassionate prophet that we

find when reading Hosea or Isaiah. Somewhat dog-matic, his objective was to convince his people that this catastrophe was a result of their sin, that Jehovah was angry with them and the only way of saving themselves was to repent of these sins. He goes on to describe "the day of Jehovah," a time when the Jews who did not follow His instruction, along with the Gentiles, would receive their reward (destruction) and the obedient Jews theirs (glorification).

Yet in the midst of all this woe, Joel offers one of the most magnificent promises in the Bible: "I will restore to you the years which the swarm-ing locust has eaten. . . . You shall eat in plenty and be satisfied, and praise the name of the Lord your God, who has dealt wondrously with you."[20]

"The years of the locust" represent those bar-ren periods in our life, those times when we feel as if we are separated from God or our good. A number of years ago, my friend Angela went through an illness in which she was told that her life was in danger. As she described it, "The doc-tors made me an offer I couldn't refuse." The sur-gery that helped to bring about a cure left Angela badly scarred, both physically and emotionally.

She might have accepted the situation in time,

but the law of compensation works in mysterious ways, adjusting itself to the specific needs of the individual. Angela discovered that plastic surgery could remove the scars and repair the deformity left by the previous surgery. Someone recently asked her how she felt during that difficult period. Angela laughingly replied that she could hardly remember. She recalled that she had been deeply troubled, but it seemed totally removed from her, almost as if these things had happened in some other lifetime.

How are lost years restored? human nature asks. How can those things that are taken be returned? In literal fact, the answer is that they cannot. But Spirit knows no time, only the eternal now. If we are expressing joy in this moment, then like Angela, we are no longer bound to the past. In Truth, it is restored. If we are experiencing happiness now, we feel no loss from a period that no longer exists, and that which appeared to be lost is returned.

Metaphysically, the "remnant" is that part of us individually which, like Noah, "walked with God."[21] Regardless of what we have been or what we have done, no matter how appalling our past might seem, within each of us there exists this "remnant" that is faithful in following Truth. Always this is preserved, and out of it the awareness of the Christ of our being is born in consciousness.

The Psalmist wrote, "This is the day which the Lord has made; let us rejoice and be glad in it."[22] This is, indeed, the day which the Lord made. And as we rejoice, it is as if "the years of the locust" had never been.

———————◄○►———————

Compensation Receptors

1. Recognize that there is no loss in Spirit. This is a law that cannot be broken. Whatever you give in love will be returned with interest. There is a Principle in this universe that knows only to manifest itself. It does this without our help or concern. Whatever act we perform immediately creates a vacuum, which this Principle rushes to fill with itself. Knowing this, it is beholden upon us to execute extreme care as to the type of vacuum we create.

2. Realize that nature overcompensates for even the appearance of loss. Emerson wrote: "As no man had ever a point of pride that was not injurious to him, so no man had ever a defect that was not somewhere made useful to him. Every man in his lifetime needs to thank his faults."[23] God is a generous Parent, and He returns to His children tenfold for any seeming lack.

3. The law is that as we think, speak, and act, we receive. If your "compensation" seems slow in arriving, speak words of welcome. Affirm that which is yours through Spirit will come to you. It will, you know, in even more wonderful ways than you expect.

4. Music has a special attracting power. What we sing is quickly and permanently assimilated into our consciousness. "I know my own shall come to me" are words of a beautiful Unity hymn.[24] Sing this affirmation joyously, knowing that your own is truly on its way to you. No power on Earth can keep it from you!

5. Act. Give of your goods and of yourself. The only sin (failure to achieve your highest po-

tential) is in doing nothing, for then there can be no compensation. Consider Jesus' Beatitudes.[25] Each blessing is followed by a specific activity. "Blessed are" those who act. The more we do, the more we give, the more we automatically receive. We need not concern ourselves with the worthiness of our recipients. How freeing this knowledge is!

PARADOXES

Chapter 4

Release

"And he rested on the seventh day."[1]

When Woodrow Wilson was President of the United States, approval of a paper was designated by the word *okeh*, followed by his initials in the margin. Someone asked why he misspelled the word, rather than using the more convenient OK. "Because that is incorrect," the President replied. He then suggested that his critic look up the word *okeh* in the dictionary. He did and discovered it to be a Choctaw Indian word meaning, "It is so."

Woodrow Wilson evidently understood that there comes a time when all that can be accomplished in the outer has been done and must be released to that greater Power who completes the job. This is the essence of release— "It is so."

The word *release* comes from the Latin *laxare* which means "to loosen." Its definition is "to set loose again; to set free from restraint, confinement, or servitude; to liberate; to free; to set at liberty."[2] We can easily visualize the joy of one being freed from prison. But how much more important is the releasing of our thoughts from the prison of our mind that they may carry out the true work assigned them.

Release is necessary to our nature. In the fifth century B.C.E., a scribe named Ezra arrived in Jerusalem, following the Babylonian exile. To his thinking, the Judean Jews had become lax in their observance of the law and needed stricter rules to live by. He thus presented them with the Priestly Code. He believed this more stringent system would benefit not only the nation, but the individual as well. Two provisions of the Priestly Code were the observance of the sabbatical year and proper reverence for the Sabbath day.[3]

The Sabbatical Year

The observance of the sabbatical year required that the land be allowed to lie fallow each seven years. *The Revealing Word* states that "the number *seven* represents fullness in the world of phenomena; *seven* refers to the divine law of perfection for the divine-natural man."[4]

Most farmers would agree that allowing the land to restore itself periodically is a good agricultural practice. Metaphysically, this means that human beings must also obey the laws in the "world of phenomena" which govern physical well-being. Jesus recognized this, for he stated that we must "render therefore to Caesar the things that are Caesar's, and to God the things that are God's."[5] To claim to be so "spiritual" that we need not concern ourselves with the physical world, or to blatantly ignore essential requirements of our body, is to fail to tend properly to that which belongs to God. My friend Herbert attempted this.

Kate, his wife, called early one morning with the news that Herbert was in intensive care at the hospital following a heart attack. "I'm just waiting to see the good that comes from this," she added almost excitedly. Kate had previously confided that she was certain God intended Herbert for the ministry. It sounded as if she thought this might be God's way of giving Herbert a nudge.

Herbert, however, had exhibited no evidence of fulfilling Kate's goal for his life. Though he accepted his wife's dedication to the study of Truth, his only outward manifestation of personal interest was the frequent invocation of God's name in something less than a reverent manner. And if Herbert was concerned with Spirit, it was spirits of a different variety.

Immediately after Kate's call, our group began prayer work. We were delighted that within a short time Herbert was home. Further tests showed no damage to his heart.

"Good" did come from this incident, though not as Kate had hoped. God was, indeed, nudging Herbert. He was telling him to take care of his body, to exercise, to cut out food and drink that added only weight and no nutrition, to treat his body as the temple that it is.

Herbert was forced by circumstance to allow his "land" to lie fallow for a season—and his was a massive "body of land," more than a hundred pounds overweight.

Kate was not mistaken in her expectation of good. Her mistake was in believing that God brought about Herbert's condition. God had nothing to do with it! It was the natural result of Herbert's ill treatment of his body. Nevertheless, out of every situation God offers the opportunity for good, if we cooperate. Herbert did, and his health has been restored.

"Remember the Sabbath"[6]

Like all the commandments, remembering the Sabbath day "to keep it holy" has an important meaning in our individual life. Traditionally, the "Sabbath" has referred to that one day out of seven, designed for churchgoing and rest. In truth, however, every day is the Sabbath, and it is as essential that we take time for daily communion with God as to nourish our physical body with food.

Some might say, "I don't have time!" We are told that Charles Fillmore spent hours each day in the silence, yet had ample time to teach, write, study, and lecture. Judging from the products of these prayer periods, we might well turn that old excuse around and say, "I don't have time *not* to pray and meditate!"

When we first attempt meditation, it may seem that nothing is happening. At first we may feel uncomfortable or perhaps too comfortable and drift into sleep. This is all right. The time will inevitably come when we discover that ideas appear precisely when we need them, that we are guided in making right decisions, that our relationships with others improve, that our health is better, that our finances increase.

Carlyle wrote, "Silence is the element in which great things fashion themselves together; that at length they may emerge, full-formed and majestic, into the daylight of life, which they are thenceforth to rule."[7]

It is good to have a specific time and place to meet with God, but eventually we see that each day is holy and all God's universe, His temple.

We then realize that our every thought, every word, every act is a prayer, and by receiving God's thoughts, we remain in constant meditation, regardless of where we are or what we may be doing.

The Garbage Collectors

"My family was always looking at the dark side of life. It seemed there had to be a villain to blame when things went wrong. The villain was closely and suspiciously observed and everything he did reported back to the family—judged, then commented upon. We didn't do anything—just talk, talk, talk! As a child, I accepted this as normal family behavior and even joined in. Then one day, I realized this was no fun at all. I felt sick. It was as if a dark brown mass of poison was floating around the pit of my stomach. I literally revolted and refused to join in. Naturally, the family didn't like that. It was like losing a drinking buddy. But I think it saved my sanity." This was the true story related by Marlene, a student in one of our classes.

Harvey's experience went like this: "We stood around the coffee pot at the office every day. Jim would say, 'Ain't the economy awful?' Then George joined in with how prices were rising. Bill expected a depression. Before long we had World War III going strong. And I was as bad as the rest! When I realized what was happening, I quit drinking coffee!"

Miriam's tale was similar: "We played bridge every week. Then one day I realized I was having headaches after every game. When I began to objectively listen to the conversation around the table I knew where those headaches came from! Sally would say, 'The neighborhood is going downhill!' Carolyn would add that she'd heard of someone who had heard of someone who had been robbed on the next block. Audrey said she'd heard the same thing, and that wasn't all. Did we know there had been a rape on the school grounds? And the worst part is that *I* was sitting there bobbing my head up and down, my mind going a mile a minute, trying to come up with a story heavier than theirs! I like bridge, but the price is too high!"

My friends were right. A change was in order. But coffee breaks and bridge were not the culprits. They merely provided the social climate where such conversations could thrive when allowed to do so. Negativity is not limited to talk. With our subliminal faculties in a near stupor, we stare in a semi-trance at television, movies, and newspapers. We listen to the radio, absorbing without question whatever trash is tossed at us.

But this is unnecessary.

We can place a watchman at the gate of our mind to accept or reject that which attempts to enter our domain.

None of us would enter a restaurant, bypass the menu, and order a large portion of garbage. Yet this is what we do with an even more delicate part of our equipment than our stomach each time we participate in such diversions as those described above. To live the abundant life of which Jesus spoke,[8] it is necessary to eliminate or renounce those thoughts which are less than uplifting. They make us ill—diseased—both physically and emotionally.

Charles Fillmore said: "Thoughts have a four-dimensional capacity. . . . Thoughts are things; they occupy space in the mental field."[9] Surely none of us wants a mental field cluttered with four-dimensional slop!

But how do we stop this infiltration of thought pollution? We combat it by the power of denial. We renounce it. It is not necessary to rise up in righteous indignation and start an argument or angrily storm from the room each time we disapprove of the tone of conversation. But we can refrain from joining in. We can avoid situations where we know this is what to expect. We can mentally deny the validity of what is being said and forbid its entry to our consciousness. And most important, we can bless the situation and affirm the Truth.

A significant way of eliminating these situations from our life is to become involved with groups of Truth-seeking people. While it is true that we are sustained by our own inner consciousness of the Christ, it is also a fact that sharing this consciousness with other persons is the highest form of human happiness. We can read, study, deny, and affirm all alone, but there is a reinforcing power in being with others who share our goals. We literally charge one another's batteries with the power of God. Truly, Truth students need each other!

Secrets Are Sacred

Another important aspect of the law of release is secrecy. Human nature tells its deepest desires, discusses its dreaded fears, confesses its clinging guilts. This is a mistake.

To randomly talk about the things closest to our heart is to dissipate our energy and enthusiasm from productive activity. We might compare our desires to a human embryo. It knows how to develop in its mother's womb without advice from the outside world. Someone asked a well-known writer what project he was currently working on. His reply was, "I am pregnant with book." That ended the discussion. Most writers know that to tell their tale prematurely is to abort their efforts.

In the same manner, to incessantly talk over challenges, fears, and guilts is to energize them, for words have power. This in no way implies that we should not turn for guidance to those who are qualified and in a position to help us. It is aimless chatter that diminishes our good and augments every dilemma.

The words *secret* and *sacred* are similar in sound. *Secret* comes from the Latin *secretes*, which means "to set apart."[10] *Sacred* comes from the Latin *sacer*, which is also the root of the word *sane*. The Greek root of *sacred* is *saos*, which means "safe."[11] In these words, we find a common idea. That which is sacred should be kept secret—safe, sane, set apart, unsullied by foolish verbosity.

Albert Einstein was asked for a mathematical formula for success in life. He offered this:

"If 'A' is 'success,' the formula is 'A=X+Y+Z,' 'X' being 'work' and 'Y' being 'play.'"

"But what is 'Z'?" he was asked.

"Keeping your mouth shut," was Einstein's reply.

Forgiveness

Forgiveness is the highest form of release. We have heard the statement, "I can forgive, but I'll never forget." This, of course, is not forgiveness. It is merely holding a grudge. As Truth students we know that when we fail to forgive, we hurt no one but ourselves. The person with whom we are angry is probably unaware that we harbor such feelings. Forgiveness is the turning loose or releasing of those persons or conditions which bind us to unhappiness. We forgive for our own well-being.

If we are experiencing lack, or if we are failing to achieve our goals, we might examine ourselves to see if there is some person or circumstance that needs releasing.

My friend Sarah had been employed by a company for more than ten years. She enjoyed her work and was on excellent terms with her fellow employees. There would likely have been no problem when she was assigned a new supervisor, had it not been that this man (call him "Mr. A") had a wife who was intensely jealous. Shortly after Mrs. A met Sarah, Sarah was "laid off" from the company.

Though Sarah immediately found a new position at an even better salary, she was deeply hurt, especially that her "friends" had not stood up for her. She knew that she should forgive, but her daydreams consisted of "telling off" those she felt had wronged her. Her bitterness grew till it was taking its toll. Her health had deteriorated. She was alone more often. And even with a larger paycheck, she was having trouble paying her bills.

Since she was unable to forgive, Sarah prayed for the *ability* to forgive. One Sunday she attended a Unity service. The lesson was "Beholding the Christ" in others. She realized that, though none of us expresses the Christ at all times, everyone has moments when the Christ light shines through.

After the service she sat quietly and brought to her memory each person toward whom she felt animosity, especially Mr. and Mrs. A. She meditated until she was able to recall an incident, regardless of how seemingly trivial, when each person had expressed some positive quality. She saw him or her smiling and happy, giving the best of self. After that, each time hurtful memories returned, she would recall these pictures and verbally affirm, "I behold the Christ in you!" Within a short time her bitterness had faded.

This is not the end of Sarah's story. One day a few months later, she received an unexpected visit from the company's vice president, the very person who, at Mr. A's request, had dismissed her. Mr. A had been transferred to another state to be near his wife with whom he was attempting a marital reconciliation. Sarah received an apology and was asked to return, not to her old position, but to a better one.

Here was the moment she had waited for— the moment when she could vent her full wrath on her persecutor! But suddenly Sarah realized how truly happy she had become. Telling this person off was no longer important. She politely thanked him, but declined his proposition. She was able, however, to offer the name of a capable friend who was looking for work. The friend applied and received the job that had been offered Sarah, and everyone benefited. Without Sarah's efforts to forgive, clearly this happy ending could never have come about.

There is a story of two Zen monks who, starting a journey one night, came upon a woman lying injured by the side of their path. It was lonely and dark, and one of them picked her up and carried her on his back till they came to an area where she could receive help. Some time went by, then the second monk turned to the first and accused, "I don't think it was right for you to carry that woman on your back." The other replied, "I carried her on my back for ten minutes, but you, my brother, have carried her for hours."

This is what we do when we hold grievances. Carrying these on our back results in ill health, poverty, and difficulty in human relationships. Naturally, it blocks all creative flow.

Each of us has done things that we regret. It is, therefore, important that we *regularly* forgive ourselves before these guilts build up. One technique for attaining self-forgiveness is to go back in our mind and, reliving the experience, mentally correct it. It is good to practice this mental erasure each night before retiring. The subconscious accepts as fact that which is presented to it vividly and with clarity. Once the amended picture is accepted, we are forgiven. God holds no grudges.

Perhaps we feel we have hurt others. The fact that we recognize our mistake and would not willingly repeat it is proof that God has forgiven us. Often we are less kind to ourselves. I recently talked with a woman, now a grandmother, who described with great emotion the guilt she still carried regarding an incident that had taken place when she was in high school!

But how do we free ourselves of these feelings? If possible, it is good mental hygiene to let the person we think we have wronged know that we regret our action. To sincerely apologize is emotionally freeing.

Often, however, an apology is impossible. When this is the case, a helpful method for accepting forgiveness is to write a letter to the individual to whom you feel indebted. Explain the circumstances of what occurred. Rewrite it, if necessary, until the letter expresses exactly what you feel. Then put it in a can and burn it. Take the ashes outside and throw them to the winds. The person may never consciously receive your message, but some part of him or her will know and understand.

This procedure can also be used if you have difficulty in forgiving yourself. Sit down and write a letter to God. Pour out your heart to Him. Tell Him how you feel. Tell God what happened and how you would like to correct it. Then, as before, burn it and release the ashes.

Jesus told us that we are forgiven as we forgive others.[12] It is not that someone's withholding of forgiveness can in any way harm us. The only harm is in our own feeling of separation from God or good. The forgiveness of which Jesus spoke enables us to remain in tune with this great law of love that heals, prospers, and harmonizes our world.

Release Mechanisms

1. The Psalmist wrote, "Rest in the Lord."[13] Relax, release, and rest in the knowledge that the Lord, the law of your being, knows how

to bring all things about. Do not try too hard. Composer Johannes Brahms told this story to a friend: "I had begun work on various compositions, but I couldn't finish them. Then I thought, oh well, I'm just too old. I then decided to write no more. I relaxed and saw in the future a happy and carefree old age to be enjoyed in peace. The idea made me so happy and contented that suddenly ideas came, and I began to write and haven't stopped since!"

2. If you are attempting to release something with which you are intensely involved, you might try the trick of trading prayers with a trusted associate. Meditate on the healing of that person's challenge and let him or her tend yours. Physicians rarely treat members of their own household. This is sometimes a helpful rule for metaphysicians as well.

3. Remember that when left alone, most problems work themselves out. It was Napoleon's habit to leave all correspondence unopened for three weeks. At the end of that time most

of it had taken care of itself. The same is true of our challenges.

4. Much is said about freeing our environment of pollution, yet how much more important it is to free our mental environment of pollution! Guard your sense faculties with care. Avoid falsehoods that attempt to impose themselves upon you. Remember the three little monkeys: "See No Evil, Hear No Evil, Speak No Evil." Follow their examples!

5. Renounce old concepts that have no validity for your life. Many of our self-imposed limitations were accepted by our subconscious when we were children and have lingered out of habit. We carry with us beliefs we would laugh at if told to us by a ten-year-old. Yet many of these were deposited by our own immature child of the past at an even earlier period in our development. Deny these false impressions and replace them with thoughts of Truth.

6. Seek the company of like-minded people. Our awareness of the true perception of re-

ality is reinforced in the company of fellow Truth seekers. Jesus said: "If two of you agree on earth about anything they ask, it will be done for them by my Father in heaven. For where two or three are gathered in my name [nature], there am I in the midst of them."[14]

7. Remember that the law of release is an active force. Longfellow wrote, "All things come 'round to him who will but wait."[15] Release is a vital step in every demonstration. It is the opposite of inactivity. To do nothing creatively takes skill. Consider a musical composition; the rests are as important as the notes. When you have done all you can, release your goal to God. It is nearer than you think.

8. Release possessiveness. You can never possess places, objects, or another person. What you do possess is their equivalent in consciousness, and this you cannot lose. You are never truly free so long as you are possessed by any *thing* less than pure love. When you willingly make this surrender, you find a paradox. You are not called upon to sacrifice that which is dear to you, but only the *hold* it has on you.

9. Forgive yourself for past errors. You are no longer the same person who made them, and you can no longer blame a person who does not exist. Affirm: *Now that I know better, I do better!*

10. If the word *forgive* implies doing something for someone you feel is not deserving, replace it with *release*. Release—both people and circumstances. There is no greater gift you can give yourself than the turning loose of grudges. Treat yourself to this gift. *You* deserve it!

Chapter 5

Nonresistance

"Do not resist."
"But overcome evil with good."[1]

My husband and I recently completed a class on the teachings of Jesus. Surprisingly, the subject of greatest interest was not the more spectacular aspects of Jesus' ministry—the miracles, the healings, the Resurrection—but, rather, the law of nonresistance. Most of the class members felt this was the principle they most needed to practice in their own lives. Delving deeper into the subject, we discovered that none of us totally understood the full impact of this marvelous law. The fact was that more often than not we *mis*understood it. In some areas where we felt we were practicing nonresistance, it became clear on closer examination that we were far from nonresistant. In other instances where we felt we were overly resistant, some of us discovered that we were, in fact, expressing nonresistance after all.

What Is Nonresistance?

Nonresistance is so important that much of Jesus' Sermon on the Mount is devoted to it, yet both Bible scholars and the general public are confused as to its real meaning. As Truth students, it is imperative that we seriously ask ourselves, "What *really* is nonresistance?" Are we expressing nonresistance when we allow others to take advantage of us? When we smile, but seethe inwardly? When we continue in a situation that has become intolerable?

Let us examine a hypothetical case, resolve it in four possible ways, then determine in which nonresistance is practiced.

John, a young man with a family, holds a responsible position for which he receives a reasonable salary. Each time there is extra work to be done, the supervisor calls on John, though others are capable of sharing the responsibility. John has never refused these additional duties, though they have often interfered with his family plans and resulted in no additional income nor hope of advancement.

On this particular occasion, John has planned a special weekend with his family. At four on Friday afternoon his supervisor approaches with a large amount of work to be completed by Monday morning.

There are several options available to John; these are a few: First, he might follow his habitual pattern—work all weekend, disappoint his family, fume quietly. Second, he could angrily refuse to do the work and perhaps quit his job. A third alternative would be for John to accept the situation as it is, quit the job, and put the past behind him. A fourth choice would allow John to remain where he is, but to get right within himself regarding his position and communicate his needs to the supervisor.

In which of these would John be practicing nonresistance?

Nonresistance Is an Attitude

Nonresistance has nothing whatever to do with what a person does. The facts regarding John's job are of no consequence. Whether or not his feelings are justified is not the issue. The way he feels about these facts is all that matters.

Neither of the first two alternatives—continuing with his job while feeling hostile or quitting in anger—is an expression of nonresistance. John could remain where he is, doing the same work. If he feels right inside, he is nonresistant regardless of the size of his workload. On the other hand, he might quit his job with the understanding that not every position is best for him, confidently knowing that he is a capable person who will find his proper place at the proper time. This, too, is nonresistance.

It is not what we do that matters. It is the way we *feel* about what we do that determines whether or not we are resistant. Feeling right, however, is not license to hurt others. The conscience is a pliable instrument and can be trained to feel no guilt. Just as pain is a warning that the body needs help, normal guilt acts as a warning that there is something in our thinking which needs to be changed. The sincere Truth student knows that a great barrier between him and his good is the false belief that he can hurt another without being hurt himself. Resistance is any attitude that places a barrier between us and our good. Nonresistance is a freeing agent that attracts good equally to ourselves and others.

In our class, we found that most of the students had the mistaken belief that "putting up with it, doing nothing to rock the boat, saying nothing," were means of practicing nonresistance. Some even felt that the more intolerable the situation one quietly endured, the more Christ-like was the individual.

As we probed this truly pragmatic philosophy, we found that nothing was further from the Truth. Jesus was a practical man and his teachings are workable. Evelyn, one of our class members, discovered that in attempting to practice nonresistance, she was being so resistant in a certain relationship that her skin was expressing her suppressed rage. The condition cleared up, along with the relationship, when Evelyn found the opportunity to come to an understanding with her friend. She came to know the beauty of Edwin Markham's "Outwitted":

> *He drew a circle that shut me out—*
> *Heretic, rebel, a thing to flout.*
> *But Love and I had the wit to win:*
> *We drew a circle that took him in.*[2]

Nonresistance is not passivity. Nonresistance is always the result of mental activity. We can be totally resistant while passively lying before an on-coming bulldozer. On the contrary, true nonresistance inevitably results in effective action. Jesus, the master of nonresistance, took the whips and drove the money changers out of the temple.[3] This was not the act of a timid, fainthearted man.

Nonresistance Is Not Escapism

The story is told of a man who called the doctor in the middle of the night insisting that he come immediately to tend his wife, who he was certain was dying from appendicitis. The doctor politely declined, but as the man persisted, he finally interrupted, "I removed your wife's appendix five years ago, Mr. Jones. She couldn't possibly have a second!"

"I know, Doctor," Mr. Jones patiently replied, "but I have a second wife!"

My friend Rosemary was much like Mr. Jones. As a child, her mother and father divorced and she lived with her mother. The father remarried. His marriage brought other children and he seldom even contacted Rosemary. Her mother's bitter words, "Men are no good!" were hard for Rosemary not to believe.

After college she married and had daughters of her own. Within a few years, however, her husband found a new love, and he and Rosemary divorced. Rosemary married a second time with the same result. A few years later she met Jim—"a wonderful Christian," she happily described him. In a short time he, too, was "straying."

Rosemary is an exceptionally attractive and talented woman. I tried to convince her that she was a person deserving love and fidelity. I also suggested that the evidence with which she was convicting Jim was exceedingly flimsy. She heard nothing I said. She could not see that her resentful suspicions and accusations were bringing about the thing she claimed not to want. "Men are no good!" she resisted, echoing her mother's words. It seemed more important to preserve the sanctity of this "family heirloom" than to save her marriage.

I do not know if Rosemary has misjudged Jim. But I do know that their marriage will continue to deteriorate until Rosemary changes the way she thinks and feels about herself and men in general. Should she divorce Jim and marry again, while still seeing her father in every man she meets, her fourth marriage will be doomed to disaster as well.

A revealing sidelight to this story is that Rosemary's daughters, like their mother and her mother before her, have followed the same marital pattern.

In other, perhaps more subtle ways, we sometimes hold to a pet peeve, a grudge, a resentment. This is resistance. To be nonresistant we must rid ourself of resentments. When we resent a person, that person clings to us. When we resent a condition, that condition draws its life from the strength of our negative attitude. How odious that we meet at every corner the very person or circumstance we find most distasteful! But this continues only until we change our thought and feeling about that person or circumstance. "Whatever you bind on earth shall be bound in heaven, and whatever you loose on earth shall be loosed in heaven,"[4] Jesus told us. If we wish to be free from any circumstance, we must first be free in that circumstance.

The words of the lawmaker Solon, "Know Thyself,"[5] were inscribed on the Delphian Temple. Recent experiments with prayer concluded that one reason many prayers appear to go unanswered is that the pray-er is praying dishonestly and with no self-understanding.[6] "In other living creatures ignorance of self is nature; in man it is vice," wrote the Roman philosopher Boethius.[7] If we hope to live a happy and fulfilling life, we cannot do as Rosemary—rationalize our misconceptions and blame others for our unhappiness. We must understand the causes of our problems and set about to overcome them. Unless we do this, we will continue to seek and find the very thing we do not want!

Resistance Leads to Inappropriate Action

A tale is told that in the ancient East there was a Sultan whose only son rushed to him, urgently requesting a horse. When asked why he was in such a hurry, the young man answered: "Death is in the garden and as I passed by, he threw out his hands to steal me away. I must have your fastest horse to escape to Baghdad!"

Sadly, the Sultan complied, and after his son was gone, he wandered alone in the garden. There he, too, came face to face with Death. "Why did you try to steal my son?" the Sultan angrily charged.

Death replied: "It was not my intent to steal him from the garden. I was so surprised to find him here that I threw up my hands in astonishment. You see, I have a tryst with him tonight in Baghdad."

The most damaging thing we can do when facing a challenging situation is to add fuel to its flame through the power of our resistance. The more we resist, the tighter we are bound by the cords of our so-called "problem." Emerson described it this way: "It seems to me that with every precaution you take against such an evil, you put yourself into the power of the evil."[8] Job lamented his fate that "the thing that I fear comes upon me, and what I dread befalls me."[9] We observe the loop in a rope. Even a child knows that the tighter each end is pulled, the tighter the loop becomes, till finally it is a full-blown knot. This same law applies to our personal challenges. The tighter we pull, the harder the knot becomes. We have to ease up, allow the threads of circumstance to relax, then take whatever action is necessary to remove the tangled situation from our life.

Ours is an action-oriented society. When in a troublesome predicament, to act is the natural human impulse. Action was primitive man's only defense against his physically superior enemies. But our job as Truth students is not to act as the "natural" man, but to act as the unnatural, the *super*natural—the Christ person.

When we react or allow ourselves to become resistant, we tie our physical and emotional selves in knots. The effect on our health is obvious. Circulation is restricted. Normal digestive processes are impeded. Breathing comes faster and with more effort. In this state, primitive man was primed for fight or flight. But we are not our primitive ancestors, and by using our wonderful mind, we have every right to expect a much longer and more productive life than they.

Resistance goes by many names. One is "impulsiveness." Norma found herself in the midst of a financial crisis. She hastily married a man she believed to have money, though she did not love or even like him. Perhaps he sensed her real feelings, for he proved to be less than generous with his funds. By the time Norma ended this ill-fated match, her financial affairs were worse than before.

Resistance can also paralyze us into foolish inactivity when action is essential. Perry lost his job and became so filled with self-pity that he refused to seek another. Before he came to his senses, he and his family suffered much unnecessary lack. Perry would not have described his nonaction as "resistance" as he sat day after day staring dejectedly through his bedroom window. But is this kind of self-centered pride not a form of resistance?

Nonresistance Acts From Strength

The use of nonresistance might seem paradoxical to the surface-thinking person. Though the effects of nonresistance are peace, tranquillity, and serenity, these come as the direct result of an inner strength, never out of weakness or cowardice. We are not practicing nonresistance when we are outwardly placid, while inwardly quaking. We are practicing nonresistance when we are willing to take whatever action is necessary for the good of all and in an attitude of love. The paradox is that when we achieve the strength to do whatever is necessary, this very strength broadcasts itself to the world and, as a result, unwanted action is rarely called for.

I recently talked with a woman who taught in a school for girls labeled "incorrigible." She said that the common factor in each life was discipline—too much or too little. The loving parents discipline their child; but as the child matures, less physical discipline is necessary and the child follows the parents' guidelines out of understanding and respect.

Woodrow Wilson, in an address in Convention Hall, said:

"The example of America must be the example not merely of peace because it will not fight, but of peace because peace is the healing and elevating influence of the world, and strife is not.

There is such a thing as a man being too proud to fight. There is such a thing as a nation being so right that it does not need to convince others by force that it is right."[10]

This is true of nations. It is true also of individuals.

May I share a personal experience? Our son Tracy and daughter Gina attended public schools at a controversial time and place. "For sale" signs appeared overnight in our area as a result of the court order to desegregate the schools. Neighbors sold their homes for a fraction of their value and hurriedly moved to the suburbs. Private schools, many not fully accredited, appeared in every available building.

Both races were fearful as each day brought new reports of what "they" were doing. "They" were either black or white, depending on the source of the rumor. Negativity was the norm as the law of the land was emotionally and physically resisted.

I brushed off the bridge table gossip, but it became personal when the terrifying stories reached home through our children. Like my husband and me, Gina and Tracy had not been taught to prejudge others nor to categorize people. Each week at Unity they attended church and Sunday school with children of all races and backgrounds and were friends with them all. Why, then, should we suddenly become apprehensive that there would be black children in what had previously been an all-white school? we asked ourselves. No decision was necessary. We saw no need for change.

Gina and Tracy were not concerned. They respected themselves and the other young people involved. They realized that the education they received was their direct responsibility, and the school merely provided the opportunity for them to learn. They were also aware that the children entering a strange, new environment and looked upon with suspicion faced a much greater challenge than they. In understanding that people sometimes become defensive under such circumstances, it was easier for them to lose the fear that had become so contagious and to turn the other cheek when tempers flared.

Even though some skirmishes took place during this adjustment period, Gina and Tracy were not involved. They discovered that understanding is also contagious. As a result, they continued to receive an excellent education, while enjoying the friendship of people from all cultures.

Though this approach seemed right for our family, I do not claim that our way is best for everyone. Had we not felt that our children were able to cope in a positive manner, we would have taken different action. Jesus told us: "If your right eye causes you to sin, pluck it out and throw it away. . . . And if your right hand causes you to sin, cut it off and throw it away."[11] To attempt to demonstrate beyond our capacity or necessity is to "tempt the Lord your God"[12] and foolishness prompted by personal ego.

Not surprisingly, we discovered that many who moved from the area to avoid busing and integration continued to move, proving again the universal law that until we face our conflicts, we continue to meet them in one guise or another.

Nonresistance Is Love

As always, we must begin with our thoughts. All growth proceeds from the calm, though never static, center that knows the Truth in fullness.

John Ruskin said: "People are always expecting to get peace in heaven; but you know whatever peace they get will be ready made. Whatever making of peace they can be blest from must be on the earth here."[13]

In Omar Khayyam's *Rubaiyat* we read:

> *I sent my Soul through the Invisible,*
> *Some letter of that After-life to spell,*
> *And by and by my Soul returned to me,*
> *And answered,*
> > *'I Myself am Heav'n and Hell.'*[14]

Our heaven begins in the mind and stretches outward into the world. We are children of God, heirs to all that the Father possesses. There is nothing for us to resist.

Nonresistance, my friend, is nothing more nor less than love.

Resistance Ridders

1. Become mentally and emotionally honest with yourself. There is no danger so great as

self-deception. When you rationalize your feelings (Certainly, I'm angry! I have a right to be! Just look what they did to me!), you build a wall so dense that your good cannot get through to you. Your indwelling Lord is not interested in *why* you think and feel as you do. He is only interested in *what* you think and feel. And your prayers are answered accordingly.

2. Recognize your so-called "evils" for what they really are—nothing, pretending to be something. Tell them so! Deny their reality. Contrary to certain unfortunate tales currently popular in motion pictures, novels, and reportedly religious writings, there is no force of evil. If there were, no power on Earth could destroy it, for Principle is unchanging. Jesus said, "You will know the truth, and the truth will make you free."[15] Affirm the Truth. Evil is a parasite, and when you refuse to act as its host, it ceases its pretense, for it has no life except that which you mentally give to it. Then as you let go of your inner conflicts, they find their own solution through dissolution.

3. It has been said that all things are possible to one who practices nonresistance. With faith, turn away from the challenge and with Epictetus, "Dare to look up to God and say, Deal with me in the future as Thou wilt; I am of the same mind as Thou art; I am Thine; I refuse nothing that pleases Thee; lead me where Thou wilt; clothe me in any dress Thou choosiest."[16] Then take appropriate, effective action in the world. We are free to do, to *be* whatever we choose.

Chapter 6

Perfection

*"You, therefore, must be perfect,
as your heavenly Father is perfect."*[1]

*In this broad earth of ours
Amid the measureless grossness and the slag,
Enclosed and safe within its central heart,
Nestles the seed of Perfection.*[2]

The great mystic-poet Walt Whitman, in his
"Song of the Universal," expressed a truth that
most of us recognize as an ideal but not as reality. We perceive that somewhere within us exists
that spark of divinity, the "seed of Perfection."
Jesus, however, said, "You, therefore, must be perfect as your heavenly Father is perfect."

For centuries Jesus' words have been brushed aside as meaning: "You really *ought* to be perfect" (a nice idea, but of course we can't attain it); or "You should *strive* to be perfect" (God appreciates our efforts, though we'll never make it); or "If you want to go to heaven when you die you'd *better* be perfect!" (but since God knows this is impossible, God sacrificed His son on a cross to take away our sins). Somewhere along the way another concept arose: "You're not perfect now, but *someday*, after this life is over, you'll be perfect" (a total change in consciousness brought about by the mere event of physical death?).

These are not the teachings of Jesus. He did not waste time on futile idealisms. He was a practical man whose purpose was to show us how to live the abundant life. He was not speaking of duty or of attempting to become something we cannot become or even of potentiality. Jesus was speaking Truth and fact—right here and now.

If there were some question as to our biological classification or species, it might be resolved thusly: "You, therefore, must be human, as your earthly parents are human." Logical? Of course. There is no question that we *ought* to be or *should* be human, or that someday, through the grace and sacrifice of our parents, we *might* achieve some degree of humanity. We *are* human. It is our nature and cannot be denied.

In this same manner, we are spiritually perfect. This, too, is our nature and cannot be denied.

A beautiful pecan tree, perhaps a hundred years old, grows in our front yard. I hold its fruit in my hand. The pecan is small, less than an inch long and a half inch in diameter. Yet as it falls to the ground, all the forces of nature begin the process that results in a pecan tree.

In your imagination, gaze with me at that tiny pecan. Hold it in your hand, then visualize the tree as it towers above our two-story home. The two look nothing alike, and we know this tree cannot return to this small protective shell that burst away so long ago. We know, too, that the tree and the pecan cannot be separated, for inherent within this pecan are all the essential elements to produce a tree. Within this pecan is an idea—the idea of a tree, a very specialized kind of tree.

The same is true of each of us. Nestled safe within our central heart is "the seed of Perfection," the idea of that very specialized spiritual being that we are.

Were you to enter a kitchen and find a cake in the process of being mixed, you would note little resemblance between the conglomeration of ingredients in the mixing bowl and the finished product. Yet most of us have taken part in this or seen its results so often that we take for granted that these seemingly unrelated items become a cake. Likewise, we look at a pecan and know that within it is the tree. Why, then, do we fail to perceive our own nature? Perhaps the reason is that we dwell in a misconception of time. It seems to take about an hour to make a cake, a few years to grow a tree, yet time beyond comprehension to perfect a human being. In Truth, there is no time, and this "seed of Perfection" planted at our "central heart" exists in fullness—*now.*

There is no conflict between the words of Whitman that we possess the "seed of Perfection" and the words of Jesus that we "must be perfect." There is no difference in the seed and its product. They are one and the same. The paradox is our inability to recognize what we are. Right now, this moment, regardless of appearance, we are as perfect as we will ever be!

What we are experiencing is an event taking place. If our awareness were expanded, we could see that what we think of as confusion, harmony, error, right judgment, chaos, positives and negatives, are only the coming together of the parts of the whole, which together make up the completed event.

We, as human beings, perceive in microscopic segments, while in Truth all things exist concurrently. If we could see beyond this experience, we would know our perfected idea in completion.

As we walk along a road, we see a small portion of the world. If we raise our vantage point by looking from the window of a building or an airplane, we observe a fuller view.

The three-dimensional senses do not grasp the totality of our being. This we perceive with an inner faculty. Space, time, and motion run parallel in the human experience. In Truth, however, they are one.

Life's Tendency

Innate within every area of our life is the tendency toward perfection. If there is discord anywhere, all the power in the universe rushes to harmonize, focusing its total attention at that point, as if it had no other purpose.

If there are approximately six billion people on this Earth,[3] our need does not receive one-six billionth of life's healing energies. Our need receives as much as we are able to accept, and there is still enough for everyone else to receive all they are able. *The Revealing Word* describes this urge toward perfection as "the spiritual seed of the Christ, which ever seeks to unfold its divine nature."[4]

We know that if we have a physical need, the physician merely provides the proper conditions for healing to take place. If a bone is broken, she sets it in the best position for the bones to knit properly together. She can bandage a wound or treat a malfunctioning organ. Yet this in itself does not heal; it merely provides the proper atmosphere by which the body follows its natural impulses toward the expression of perfection.

When I was nine years old, I experienced a

graphic demonstration of this power in a way I will never forget. A large, ugly wart suddenly appeared on the knuckle of the index finger of my right hand. It was a constant source of embarrassment, for when we played games at school, holding hands, it was in the exact position to be noticed. Someone would invariably remind me (as if I could forget), "Ooooooh, you have a wart!"

One day as I stared dejectedly at the wart, I decided once and for all that I did not want it. My thinking and feeling natures were in total agreement that there was absolutely nothing to be said in favor of that wart. I had been much impressed in Sunday School by the story of how Jesus spat upon the ground and made clay, then anointed the blind man's eyes with it, thus restoring his vision.[5] If such an act could restore sight, I reasoned, surely it could remove a wart! Quietly, I withdrew to the back of the garage where I would not be disturbed. I prayed with childlike fervor, spat in the dirt, and lavishly applied mud to the wart. I then covered it with a Band-Aid and promptly forgot it. I told no one, and if anyone noticed the Band-Aid, they said nothing. Most nine-year-olds had bandages here and there. Under these circumstances, it was easy to forget. With no one to remind me, I no longer viewed myself as the possessor of a wart.

I do not recall how long the Band-Aid remained on my hand, but when I removed it the wart was gone and the skin beneath was smooth and flawless. Even at so early an age, I felt a kind of awe at what had transpired and was keenly aware that a principle had been applied and had worked.

I have recalled this incident many times since. There was surely no healing power in that filthy bandage. The power came from my unequivocal decision to be rid of the wart, from my childlike faith in prayer, and from the fact that with the bandage covering it, my attention was diverted from the wart. Left alone with no one to remind me of it, the restorative power of nature was free to perform its perfecting work.

The same restorative power is at work, not only in our physical bodies, but in every area of our lives. It expresses as abundance, creativity, love, wholeness. Its sole purpose is to pour itself out and harmonize. It knows how to heal every infirmity and discord, and we can only deter its action through our interference. This power is not only willing, but desires to apply all of its energies to the purpose of perfecting, regardless of what the need might be.

Are We Lying to Ourselves?

I am healthy. Every part of my body—physically and mentally—is vibrant and strong.

I am wealthy. I have access to all the substance in the universe. My every need is met.

I am creative. Ideas are mine through divine inspiration. I am guided and directed at all times.

I am loved and I am loving. Everyone likes me, and I see only good in others. My relationships are harmonious and joyful.

How do you feel about these statements? Can you speak them with authority and assurance, or do you feel a twinge, a sense that you are not being quite honest with yourself?

"How can I say, 'I'm healthy,' when I'm in pain and the doctors say my condition is hopeless?" someone might ask. "How can I say, 'I'm wealthy,' when I'm in debt and don't know where my next meal is coming from?" "How can I say, 'I'm creative,' when my mind is so muddled that no constructive thought could possibly find its way through this miasma of confusion?" "How can I say, 'I'm loved and loving,' when my life is falling apart?"

The seeker of Truth inevitably asks these or similar questions and in turn is asked them by others. We learn that we affirm and give thanks that we now have that which we desire, though it may appear far from factual. To claim our good loudly and forcefully is difficult for many, for it may appear that we are attempting to fool ourselves. There is, however, a law at work and when we make these claims, we call our good from the invisible to the visible, from the ideal to the manifest. As we see the results, we never again hesitate to make use of this affirming power, which literally draws inner perfection into the outer world.

Robert Browning beautifully illustrates this in these words from his poem, "Paracelsus":

> *Truth is within ourselves; it takes no rise*
> *From outward things, whate'er you may*
> *   believe.*
> *There is an inmost center in us all,*

Where truth abides in fulness . . .
    and to know
Rather consists in opening out a way
Whence the imprisoned splendor may
    escape,
Than in effecting entry for a light
Supposed to be without.[6]

Me Vs. I

When we make such statements as *I am healthy, wealthy, inspired, and loved,* we are not referring to "me," the personality; but rather to "I," the perfect idea, the seed, the I AM of God planted in each of us.

In *Lessons in Truth,* H. Emilie Cady describes it this way:

> *Personality* applies to the human part of you—the person, the external. It belongs to the region governed by the intellect. . . . It is the outer, change-able man, in contradistinction to the inner or real man. *Individuality* is the term used to denote the *real* man.[7]

We must realize that the true "I" (individuality) is always at unity with the Father, the Source of all good. Therefore, when I say that "I, the child of God, am all and have all," I am speaking the Truth about myself. As soon as I am able to convince "me," the personality, that this is true, then it becomes a fact in the world of phenomena as well.

That which we refer to as "fact" is subject to change. Paul said, "For now we see in a mirror dimly . . . . Now I know in part."[8] It may be a fact that we are experiencing an inharmonious situation, but this is relative. It is not eternal. When we move to the realm of the Absolute, we can claim with perfect confidence, "I am health; I am wealth; I am inspiration; I am love," because this is the eternal Truth about each of us. If this were not true in the Absolute, then no one could hope to be healed, to overcome poverty, to express creatively, or to find happiness.

A Household of "I's"

We are never our true Self as a personality, only as an individual. Personality dwells on appearances; individuality dwells on Truth. Individuality is One, the I AM; personality may be composed of several or even thousands of parts.

The Russian esoteric psychologists Gurdjieff and Ouspensky[9] taught that we must learn to differentiate between "I" and "it" or, as Dr. Cady defined it, "individuality" and "personality."

We are all familiar with the more sensational cases of multiple or split personalities. They are striking and make the news, yet each of us has multiple personalities. As we observe ourselves, we find that we are composed of many false "I's." The only difference between us and these spectacular cases is the degree to which we have integrated these personalities into our consciousness as a unity. Perhaps a writer of Proverbs was aware of this psychological quirk when he wrote, "He who troubles his household will inherit wind."[10]

The word *personality* comes from the Latin *persona,* which refers to "a face mask used by actors on the stage; hence a character, a person."[11] We can easily see that we wittingly or unwittingly put on varied masks, depending upon the circumstances. We wear one mask with our children, another with our spouse, another with a casual acquaintance. I am acquainted with one young woman, married and with a family, who literally reverts to baby talk when in the presence of her overly solicitous mother.

To be in control of ourselves as a total entity, we must refuse to allow our "I," our real Self, to become entwined with unproductive personalities. They are not "I." We should merely observe them, practice nonresistance, and allow them to fade naturally from our lives.

Pull Yourself Together!

I had the opportunity to return to college for my degree after nineteen years of marriage and with two children in school. One of the courses offered was designed to help the student gain self-knowledge. Our main assignment was to objectively observe ourselves and keep a daily journal describing the activities of the false "I's." For one semester about twelve of us followed this intriguing regimen, meeting for three hours once a week to discuss the "I's" with whom we were becoming acquainted.

We discovered that there were characters

(characteristics) dwelling within our consciousness of which we had had absolutely no knowledge. We were instructed to give them a name, that they be totally differentiated from the true "I." For instance, we would not say, "*I* am mad about . . ." but rather, "She/he (or the 'name') was angry that . . ." Often the name that "felt right" corresponded to the time in our lives when this particular trait or "character" developed.

These are a few examples of "boarders" in conflict with their "householder":

Jerry wanted better health, yet we rarely saw him without a fever or a sprained ankle, and more often than not, he was unable to attend class at all. He discovered a "family member" with tendencies toward illness. He gave him the name, "Sonny Boy," the nickname by which Jerry had been known at the particular time in his life when "being sick" gained him so much attention.

Debbie was constantly struggling against depression. She recognized "Mary," named in memory of the girl who had been the "teacher's pet" in the first grade. Debbie realized that she had been carrying "Mary" with her for over fifteen years. "Mary" was the perfect child. She was perfect at school. She was perfect at home. But Debbie was twenty-one years old and Mary's attempts at pleasing were geared to the first-grade level, thus doomed to disaster and resulting depression.

Kathy was the senior class president and a candidate for class valedictorian, yet she expressed serious doubts as to her capabilities and admitted that she actually suffered before each class. The prospect of looking for work after graduation was terrifying. One day she discovered "Ellen" lurking about. She suddenly realized that Ellen, her real sister, had always belittled her in subtle ways, insinuating that she was prettier, smarter, and more lovable than Kathy. That inner voice she had heard most of her life, in reality, belonged to "Ellen."

As we became aware of the presence of these "personalities" and the immaturity and inappropriateness of their demands, most of them receded and were no longer dominant characters. In the household of our mind, we also observed many "residents" who were beneficial. To be good landlords, we integrated these positive residents into the "I," while gently but firmly evicting the undesirables.

The Eye and the "I"

The development of the "I" has been the subject of allegorical teachings of all religions. We find it running through both the Old and New Testaments and in much of the teachings of Jesus.

Consider some of Jesus' statements, and by merely changing the spelling of one word, reflect on their meaning: "If your eye [I] is sound, your whole body will be full of light; but if your eye [I] is not sound, your whole body will be full of darkness."[12] Contemplate this question: "Why do you see the speck that is in your brother's eye [I], but do not notice the log that is in your own eye [I]? Or how can you say to your brother, 'Let me take the speck out of your eye [I]' when there is the log in your own eye [I]?"[13]

Consider the challenge: "If your eye [I] causes you to sin, pluck it out and throw it away; it is better for you to enter life with one eye [I] than with two eyes [I's]."[14]

Each of us has a consciousness with "inhabitants," embodying various concepts and attitudes, some far more deeply entrenched than others. The truth is that when we speak of "I," all too often we are attaching to this perfect essence something less than perfection. We must not allow our "I" to become entangled with unsavory members of our community. They are not "I." They are subjective thought personages, members of our household, welcome only when they comply with the rules that "I," the householder, decide are good and true.

The At-one-ment

The word *atone*[15] comes from a Middle English word that literally means "at one" or "agreed." We in Unity believe in the "at-one-ment" or "agreement" that Jesus established between himself and God. He can truly and with our deepest love be called "the Christ," not because he died as an expiation for our sins, but because he so totally expressed his divinity, his oneness with God, that there was no separation between the personality, Jesus, and the individuality, Christ.

We, however, cannot merely "take the name of Jesus" (that is, pay lip service) and let that be the end of it. We take the name of Jesus by taking on the *nature* that he expressed. As we seek to unify our humanity with our Christhood, as Jesus did, we too realize our at-one-ment with the Father. This results in a much different quality of life. This is the kingdom of heaven within us[16]—not in some future time and distant place, but right here and now.

The "kingdom of heaven," as Jesus used the term, refers to the idea of expansion. He used examples of growth such as the mustard seed,[17] the leaven,[18] and the treasure hidden in the field[19] to describe it. The kingdom of heaven, according to Jesus, is far from static. It is not like the ocean consuming the drop of water, but, paradoxically, like the single drop engulfing the entire ocean. It is like each person involving and absorbing all creation within his or her own individuality.

This is what Jesus did. He totally involved himself with life. All things that did not conform with the perfect God-idea of humanity, he cast aside. He saw the universe as a unity of perfection, and himself—not only as a "brother" of humankind—one with all creation. Through love, all conflicts were overcome, and Jesus, the man, became Jesus, the Christ.

The Christ indwells you and me as it did

Jesus. It is the perfect and true Self of each of us. That part of our humanity which corresponds to the Christ is eternal. The masks, the "persona," fall away.

We are, therefore, perfect as our heavenly Father is perfect.

Perfection Practice

1. Remember that you are perfect. It is inevitable, your nature, the Truth about you. Accept this as a fact in your life *now*. Charles Fillmore taught that Jesus' life was the normal standard for all and any lesser expression of life was abnormal.[20] Jesus himself told us that everything he did, we could do also.[21]

2. Recognize those attitudes of thought and emotion that hinder your expression of the perfection that you are. Deny their validity. They are nothing hiding behind the mask of something. Rip off those masks! Insist, "This is not 'I'!"

3. Affirm the Truth about yourself: *I am a per-*

fect spiritual being, joyously experiencing the wonderful human state. Remember, I AM is the name of God. "You shall not take the name of the Lord your God in vain."[22] Anything less than perfection attached to the I AM is misusing this holy name with which you are entrusted.

4. Allow this perfection to express in your life as health, prosperity, joy, love. The purpose of becoming aware of our innate perfection is not for the contemplation of abstract theories or to indulge in effortless egocentricities. It is that we, like Jesus, may express life more abundantly.

5. Act as if you are perfect. If you slip, do not kick yourself. Pick yourself up and try again.

Know this, O man, sole root of sin in thee
Is not to know thine own divinity![23]

SPIRALS

Chapter 7

Order

Spring comes early to our home in Texas. By late February an aura of green, more sensed than seen, surrounds the trees behind our house. By March the neighbors are gathered in their yards, vigorously attacking weeds, planting seeds, tending shrubs and lawns. A feeling of excitement, a promise of impending joy is in the air.

> *For lo, the winter is past,*
> *the rain is over and gone.*
> *The flowers appear on the earth,*
> *the time of singing has come,*

and the voice of the turtledove
is heard in our land. [2]

Alexander Pope said that "order is heaven's first law."[3] *The Revealing Word* describes order as "the first law of the universe. Indeed, there could be no universe unless its various parts were kept in perfect order. The facts of Spirit are of spiritual character and, when understood in their right relation, they are orderly. Orderliness is law and is the test of true science."[4]

The dictionary defines *order* as "the sequence or arrangement of things or events, series, successions; a fixed or definite plan, systematic law of arrangement; a state of condition in which everything is in its right place and functions properly."[5]

This is the way of nature. It is orderly. Imagine the chaos that would result if we could not depend on the length of days or the sequence of seasons. This does not happen.

Nature's reliability is illustrated in a story about Mark Twain. As he and a friend were leaving church, a great downpouring of rain began. "Do you suppose it will stop?" asked the worried friend. "It always has," Twain replied with calm assurance.

We can as readily place our confidence in life's natural orderliness: Jesus said, "On earth as it is in heaven."[6] The condition of our outer world is always the perfect outpicturing of our inner world. If we do not like the picture we see, we can change it by going within and putting our thoughts and feelings in order.

Health, Prosperity, Success, and Love

From the life and teachings of Jesus, four basic needs appear to have been recognized by him as essential to the abundant life. We must be healthy in body, mind, and emotions. We must have sufficient prosperity. We must express our creativity in positive ways. We must experience loving relationships with others.

The Gospels tell of many instances in which Jesus healed the sick.[7] This was a large part of his ministry. We read of his miracles of supply, such as the feeding of the 5000[8] and the turning of the water into wine at the wedding in Cana.[9] Much of his teaching, as in the parables of the talents,[10] contains the idea of constructively using that which we have been given. The very life of Jesus is an example of one who was in love with God and his fellow humankind. When asked which commandment was the greatest, Jesus' answer was, "You shall love the Lord your God with all your heart, and with all your soul, and with all your mind. . . . And a second is like it, You shall love your neighbor as yourself."[11]

Health, prosperity, creative expression, and love . . . There are innumerable variations and combinations derived from these basic needs, but difficulties can almost without exception be traced to a disorder in one of these.

Disorders

It is interesting how little attention we pay to the meaning of the words we speak. If we face a challenge, the words we use to describe it often define it as well. Consider the word *disorder.* We hear someone say that he or she is suffering a particular disorder, but do we really grasp the full implication of what has been said?

In the dictionary, we find that the prefix *dis* denotes "separation, negation, or reversal."[12] It is factual, then, that a *disorder* is a lack of order in some part of life. The solution? Restore *order* to the area where it is lacking.

Disorders can exist anywhere. A health disorder is called "dis-ease," or if less severe, "discomfort." When mental or emotional, it might be described as "dis-orientation." Someone lacking prosperity is referred to as "disadvantaged." One who fails to achieve his or her goals may become "dis-appointed" or "discouraged." A person facing challenges with another may speak of having a "dis-agreement" or being "dis-contented" in a situation. The result may be "dis-solution" or "dis-integration" of that relationship.

We receive other clues from words with the prefix *in*, meaning "no, not, and without."[13] One who is not up to par physically or emotionally may be referred to as having an "indisposition" or being "in-capacitated." Someone lacking funds to meet a need is experiencing "in-sufficiency." A person not fully expressing abilities may be called "in-effective." An unhappy relationship is "in-harmonious."

If the word defines the problem, then the solution to the healing of these disorders is also within the word. If we have a health disorder, we should contemplate the need for *ease* and *comfort,* for a true sense of *orientation* or direction in our life, for improving our *disposition* and thinking in terms of our *capacity* to live the full life. We might affirm: *I am "capable" and "predispositioned" for "ease" and "comfort" in my body, thoughts, and emotions. I am "oriented" toward that which is good.*

If we have a disorder in the area of prosperity, we can reverse this concept and think of ourselves as *advantaged,* rather than poor, then start affirming that there is *sufficient* supply to meet our demands. We could say: *I have every "advantage," and there is "sufficient" substance for me to live as the child of God that I am.*

If we appear to fail in the expression of our capabilities and desires, we should think of ourselves as meeting the *appointment* to which our Father assigned us and taking *courage* in our continuing efforts. We can affirm: *I am "effective and efficient" in all that I do. I "courageously" go forward to meet my "appointed" good.*

When working to heal disorders in our relationships with others, the method is the same, whether for the healing of a broken marriage or a minor dispute with a casual acquaintance. We find areas of *agreement* and *contentment.* We apply *harmony* to the situation. We affirm love, knowing there is no condition so serious that love cannot heal. We state: *I am "content" in the "agreement" that both you and I are expressions of life. We find our "solution" by "integrating" our differences "harmoniously."*

Cause of Death—Psychosomatic

Almost everyone today is aware of the study of psychosomatic medicine, the branch of science that uses a psychological approach in determining the cause and treatment of physical disorders. The word *psycho* comes from the Greek *psyche,* which means "soul or mind."[14] *Soma* is a Greek word for "body."[15] A psychosomatic disorder is, therefore, one "originating in or aggravated by the psychic or emotional processes of the individual."[16]

Most medical doctors readily admit that a majority of their patients are suffering from psychosomatic ailments. I recently heard a physician say that as much as 98 percent of disease originates in the mind. If this is true, what of the remaining 2 percent?

Is it possible that all disease is of psychosomatic origin and every death certificate should list as "Cause of Death"—*psychosomatic?*

Many people have the misconception that to say a disease is psychosomatic is to imply that the patient is imagining or pretending to be ill. Nothing is farther from the truth.

The fact that these patients are suffering from mind-induced ailments in no way lessens their suffering. The pain and bodily degeneration are real: that death occurs is also real. This does not alter the fact, however, that the disorder originated not organically, but in the mind.

Myra

Myra's story is typical of the manner in which disease can begin and grow. As a child, she developed a cough, which resulted in much attention from her doting parents. It happened again with the same result. Then one day when things were not going to Myra's satisfaction, she deliberately began to cough. Her fearful parents reacted as before, showering her with attention. Myra had discovered the way to control them.

A conscious pattern developed. Things went wrong. Myra coughed. She got what she wanted and stopped coughing. This went on for some time. Finally, Myra's frantic parents took the child to be examined by a physician, who diagnosed her as "asthmatic." The doctor told not only her parents, but Myra as well, that the attacks would increase in frequency and intensity, and she would be ill for the rest of her life. The only thing to be done was for Myra to avoid stress and overexertion.

Myra was not concerned. She was still the initiator of these attacks, though once they began, it became difficult to stop them. In high school she had a ready excuse to avoid activities she did not enjoy; though, to her mother's amazement, Myra could dance "till the wee hours of the morning without even a hack!"

At home Myra was exempt from even the simplest chore—nor would anyone dare cross her. About this time Myra noticed that certain outside situations seemed to trigger the onset of these attacks.

Myra married and became a mother. At this point, had she realized the seriousness of the situation, she might have eliminated it. Unfortunately, the attacks served a purpose. Though they came with greater frequency, especially when she was upset, Myra was young and otherwise strong, and each attack gained attention and privileges—now from her husband.

Then one day her husband was no longer with her and her children were grown. But the attacks were there and out of control. Myra panicked as she struggled for each breath. She was taken by ambulance to the hospital where a specialist in respiratory disease diagnosed her condition as "emphysema," brought on by the long-term effects of asthma. The doctor prescribed injections to relieve the symptoms, but warned that these drugs, taken over a long period, could damage her heart. Myra's immediate concern was each breath. Some future disaster paled by comparison.

Over the next few years Myra's condition degenerated rapidly. She was in her fifties when she died, though most of her friends thought she was older. The cause of death was given as "heart failure." Only a few knew that a little girl, some fifty years before, had chosen a course of action which led to death.

Psychosomatic Poverty, Psychosomatic Failure, Psychosomatic Alienation

If we can accept the concept that the origin of physical, mental, and emotional disorders is primarily in the mind, then what of poverty, failure, and the inability to get along with others? These are no less diseases and disorders. Might they be psychosomatic as well?

Where but in the mind does poverty begin? There is no germ, no bacteria, no virus that carries poverty. It is not organic in origin. Some might suggest heredity and cite as proof generations of welfare recipients. Though this sometimes occurs, it is not due to genes but to attitudes passed on for generations. If there were a poverty gene, then if born in want, no person could hope to rise above his natal circumstance. Yet all of us know of countless persons who have conquered privation to achieve fortunes.

If illness and poverty are psychosomatic disorders, where but in the mind does failure begin?

There are no microorganisms to carry it. Some might blame fate or our environment (a currently popular scapegoat), but we in Truth know that outside powers do not control our destinies.

Where but in the mind does alienation among individuals begin? It is said that more people fail to succeed in their work due to inability to get along with associates than from lack of qualifications or poor job performance. This is "dis-ease," as surely as is a malfunctioning organ.

Do we want to control our lives? We, alone, make the decision. If the cause of our difficulties comes from a disordered mind, then the cure is within the ordered mind. We cannot say, "His ulcer might be psychosomatic, but not my weak heart!" or "Physical problems may be psychological, but the fact that I've lost six jobs this year is just bad luck!"

If we can affirm and believe with Myrtle Fillmore *"I am a child of God and therefore I do not inherit sickness,"*[17] we can surely paraphrase her statement and affirm with equal certainty, *I am a child of God and therefore I do not inherit poverty, failure, or a bad disposition!*

Either we have control over our lives, or this is not a law and we must resign ourselves to being tossed about by every wind of chance. Either we take responsibility, or we do not.

The good news is that what the mind creates, it can recreate! This is order.

Reestablishing Order—Take Command!

Another definition of *order* is "to instruct; to direct; to command."[18] We might think of our mind as possessing an executive officer, a "general," and of the various departments of life as our branches of service. If one branch is functioning improperly, it is up to the general to control "his" troops and direct that order be established.

We cannot hope to have physical and mental health if we fail to follow the rules that govern our bodies. We must eat properly, exercise regularly, and achieve a balance in work and play.

Charles Fillmore wrote: "If we desire to demonstrate health . . . we must order this life rightly. If it is not so ordered, mental and physical discord will ensue. This applies to all that we think and do. Everything must be brought in order."[19]

A few years ago it became necessary for our thirteen-year-old dog Penny to have major surgery. Arrangements were made for our family to visit her following her operation so she would not feel afraid or lonely. Waiting for someone to take us to the kennel, I glanced through the door. Much to my surprise, there was Penny casually strolling down the hall. She looked up, saw me, and happily wagged her tail. I had expected a weak, listless animal, pathetically lying on her bed in pain. This had been the appearance of human friends recuperating from the same operation. Yet here was Penny, less than six hours after surgery, delighted to see us and eager to go home. With no one to tell her how she was supposed to feel, nature had taken charge and, without interference, had gone about its healing work in the fastest and most efficient manner.

On our local educational television station, I watched a documentary film pertaining to the power of the mind. It included a man who walked on live coals. When his feet were examined, except for being somewhat tougher, they were no different than the average and in no way damaged. Asked how he tolerated the pain, he explained that pain was merely a disorientation of the mind and when his thoughts and emotions were in order, he felt no pain.

Orderly thoughts and emotions are equally important if we hope to achieve creative and financial goals. Truth students sometimes attempt this through prayer and visualization alone, expecting God to do the rest. A third step—action—is equally important.

Horace Mann said, "Genius may conceive, but patient labor must consummate." Emerson wrote, "Every artist was first an amateur." Edison admitted: "Genius is one percent inspiration and ninety-nine percent perspiration. I never did anything worth doing by accident, nor did any of my inventions come by accident; they came by work."[20]

Too often we declare, "Divine order," then wait for the "Divine" to do all the work. This is neither divine nor orderly.

The happiest people in the world are those who "work" at the thing they love. Nor does it matter what their work might be. One of the most joyous and creative persons I know is a housekeeper.

Each day she cleans someone else's home, yet no painter or musician could receive more pleasure or satisfaction than Catherine as she polishes a floor or makes the silverware gleam. Being paid is a bonus for those who do the work they love. Remuneration, however, is inevitable, for love works so well!

Order in our dealings with others cannot be overemphasized. To attempt to untangle the twisted web of disorderly relationships would require many books, rather than a small portion of one chapter. To say that we must apply love may appear an oversimplification, yet it is the technique that works.

"Let us love one another," wrote the author of the first letter of John.[21] By "love," however, we do not mean that possessive, restrictive, sick-sweet emotion too often masquerading as love. Love does not mean giving in to another's every whim; nor does it mean becoming subservient, either physically or emotionally. Love is strong, and the constructive expression of love can be the most difficult of courses to follow.

Though love is the only answer to the challenge of inharmonious relationships, this in no way implies that we must attempt to arrive at total agreement at all times on every subject with another person. As a musical composition has melody and counter melody, changes in rhythm and tempo, an accidental here and there, the same is true in fulfilling relationships with others. It is neither necessary nor desirable that others always think as we do—not even our spouse or children (*especially* not our spouse or children!). We should not walk in one another's shadows. Differences of opinion add flavor to life. Love is knowing that each person has the Spirit of God within—just as we do—and deserves our respect and the freedom to express this Spirit in his or her own unique way.

The apostle Paul in one of his letters to the Corinthians[22] compared our relationships with one another to the interrelationship of the parts of the body. Each organ has its own function and is dependent on the others. Yet no organ is more important than another, nor can it function alone.

So it is with us. We are each an idea in the Mind of God, a member of the Christ principle. Every individual has a function, and all are essential to the expression of God's whole creation.

As each takes the responsibility for his or her

own life and recognizes the Christ, the real Self, in other persons, order is automatically established.

> *Drop Thy still dews of quietness, till all*
> *   our strivings cease;*
> *And let our ordered lives confess the*
> *   beauty of Thy peace.*[23]

Seedtime and Harvest

A story is told of two goldfish that were swimming about when one suddenly announced he was no longer certain that there was a God. "That's interesting," replied the other, "but if there's no God, who do you suppose changes the water in our bowl?"

A more famous agnostic, Robert Ingersoll, visiting Henry Ward Beecher one day, admired the clergyman's beautiful globe portraying the constellations and stars. "This is exactly what I've been searching for," Ingersoll exclaimed with delight. "Tell me! Who made it?"

"Who made it?" Beecher repeated with a twinkle in his eye. "Why, no one made it. It just happened!"

I recently read an article reporting that Robert Jastrow, an agnostic astronomer in charge of the U.S. Institute for Space Studies, believes that astronomy, rather than disproving the existence of God, is finding evidence that God exists. "There is a kind of religion in science," Jastrow says. "It is the religion of a person who believes there is order and harmony in the universe."[24]

Order and harmony . . . We observe them everywhere. But those who seek Truth know that the law and order of nature are but reflections of the One who created the universe and everything in it. Order, harmony, and nature are the effects, not the Cause.

Order is man's servant. In the bleak days of winter, we must sometimes remind ourselves that spring will return. There are times in our lives when we seem to experience a wintertime of the soul. Then, more than ever, we should remember that spring inevitably follows, and the seed that we plant in the springtime of our consciousness will one day bear fruit. The order of our life determines the fruit we reap at harvesttime.

———————◀○▶———————

Order Organizers

1. "Order is heaven's first law." This is Truth. If there is some portion of your life less than productive, inspect your "troops" like a good "general" to ensure orderliness and increased productivity in their ranks.

2. Order in your life is natural. The practice of disorder is depleting and requires far more energy than orderliness. According to *The Revealing Word*,[25] "The divine idea of order is the idea of adjustment, and as this is established in man's thought, his mind and affairs will be at one with the universal harmony."

3. Remember that one person's disorder is not necessarily another's. A cluttered desk, or a yard growing dandelions instead of grass, is not irrefutable proof of a disordered mind. You, alone, determine for yourself what order is.

4. Affirm: *I experience perfect circulation, perfect*

assimilation, and perfect elimination in every aspect of my life. I give that which I have to give, and good flows back to me; I keep that which is needful; I rid myself of that which is no longer beneficial to my well-being. Deliberately change words that describe "dis-order" to those which define "order."

5. Deny obstructions, greed, blockages, wherever they are. Nature's way is to utilize what it needs, to give generously, and to be free from that which is no longer usable. Get rid of nonessentials or nature will dispose of them for you!

6. Call on "Divine order," and watch miracles take place!

7. Do something constructive about "disorder." It is easy to determine where disorder exists. It exists in those areas where you are not expressing your full potential. "All things should be done decently and in order," wrote Paul.[26] Actively and joyously replace disorder with order!

Chapter 8

Creative Expression

"In the beginning God created . . . ."[1]

Gerda was nine years old. She was a typical little girl in most ways. She liked to play dolls and games with other children, but Gerda was different in a way that would forever change her life. She lived in Poland, and she was Jewish. Hitler had just come to power. Gerda was one of 200 girls of 4000 people who survived the death march from Germany to Czechoslovakia. When she kissed her parents good-bye, it was for the last time. They were sent to Auschwitz where they were killed.

"It's spring now," Gerda told a reporter recently. "I remember we used to stand for roll call for hours. The camp was cement, drab, gray. One day through the concrete a flower poked its head, and that flower became the most important thing in my life. You have no idea how much joy that flower gave me."[2]

A flower growing through concrete . . . How often have we walked along and observed a flower or perhaps a weed pushing its way through a broken spot in the sidewalk? How powerful is life's urge to express itself! If there is a way, a single crack in the armor, love's creative force will find it.

If a simple flower has within it this tremendous need to express, then what of the human being? For six years Gerda struggled to stay alive. "We were always hungry. We were always cold. But I wanted to live, with every fiber of my being."

How incredibly powerful is the force of life in human beings!

What Is Creativity?

The story of the first creative endeavor is told in the book of Genesis. It is God's nature to create, to express Himself. So it is with us. Creative expression is as necessary to the human being as food or air. Without it, we may exist, but not fully live. Creativity, evidenced in a variety of expressions, is God's own manifesting power working through us. God cannot express in this world except through His creation.

During World War II, a beautiful cathedral in Europe was destroyed in a bombing attack. Later, as the people went through the rubble, they came across a statue of Jesus buried beneath the debris. It was intact except for the hands, which were missing. Though the statue could have been repaired easily, it was left as it was as a reminder that God has no hands to do His work but ours.

We are goal-oriented beings. Planted within each of us is a force urging us toward greater creative accomplishment. We may think of a painter or a poet as being "creative," but creativity is not limited to those persons in the arts. Creativity is expression of any kind that brings joy to ourselves and others.

What is more creative than giving birth to a child or tending that child as he or she grows? A businessperson offering a needed service for the public good is expressing creatively. The police officer, the teacher, the fireman, the nurse . . . the list is endless. Nor is it necessary that our creativity be expressed in salaried occupations. Retired persons can be as creative as those employed, when they are giving themselves in joy. A volunteer worker or a person involved in a much-loved hobby is expressing creatively.

"Am *I* creative?" we might ask ourselves.

The answer lies not in what we do, but rather in the way we feel about what we do. If we are performing what appears the lowliest of tasks and doing it with love and pride, then God is expressing His creativity through us. If we are composing the most beautiful symphony without joy, it is merely a chore.

> *Work thou for pleasure—paint, or sing,*
>   *or carve*
> *The thing thou lovest, though the body*
>   *starves—*
> *Who works for glory misses oft the goal;*
> *Who works for money coins his very soul.*
> *Work thou for the work's sake, then,*
>   *and it may be*
> *That these things shall be added unto thee.*[3]

Mind, Idea, Expression

The law of creativity takes place in three steps: mind, idea, and expression. There must be mind to conceive an idea. The idea then expresses in the manifest world of form. Through these steps, God created the universe. We, who are made in God's image, duplicate this process in our individual creative endeavors.

In *Mysteries of Genesis*, Charles Fillmore comments:

> It is found that what is true in the creation of the universe (as allegorically stated in Genesis) is equally true in the unfoldment of man's mind and body, because man is the microcosmic copy of the "Grand Man" of the universe.[4] The whole Genesiac record is an allegory explaining just what takes place in the mind of each individual in his unfoldment from the idea to the manifest.[5]

We are mind. We *have* a body. We were mind before we had a body, and mind will continue long

after this body ceases to function. Though the
brain and mind are often confused, they are not
the same. The brain is our physical instrument, a
kind of transmitter that the mind uses. The brain
is to the mind as the calculator is to its operator.
The brain may be damaged or even die without
affecting the mind in any way. Our mind is our
individual use of the one Mind through which we
receive ideas directly.

Emerson wrote, "When the master of the universe has points to carry in his government he
impresses his will in the structure of minds."[6] Astronomer Johannes Kepler exclaimed, "O God, I
am thinking Thy thoughts after Thee!"[7]

The Mind of God constantly thinks, and
those thoughts are projected to our minds as ideas.
Ideas are the seeds of the mind. As the acorn is to
the oak, so is the idea to the mind. Ideas are from
God and always good. When it appears otherwise,
it is because we have misinterpreted God's message and, with our marvelous power to mold substance, misprojected the original God-idea.

Everything that exists was first an idea. Fillmore continues, "God makes all things in His
mind first, which is involution; then they are made

into form and shape, and this is evolution."[8] The chair we sit upon was first an idea in mind, then formed out of universal substance into matter and molded in manifestation as a chair.

In the example of the oak and acorn, the acorn is planted in the earth and a tree is produced. Within that acorn (idea) was a generative center that, when planted in the earth (substance), produced the pattern inherent within that seed-idea.

It is not necessary for the acorn to understand the complex theories behind its creative activity. It is enough for it to *be* creative.

So it is with us. To *be* creative is our goal, and if any of us is expressing creativity to the fullest, experiencing happiness, health, and prosperity without qualification, then to study the workings of the creative process might be unnecessary.

Go forth and *be!*

Most of us, however, have not yet arrived at this ideal state. By understanding the principles of creation, we become better able to form those expressions that result in happiness for ourselves and others. If the expression is not to our liking, we know we can change it by replacing the parent thought with a new and true thought.

To sum up: God is Mind. Mind thinks. Thoughts are ideas. We are receptors for divine ideas. We translate these ideas into concepts that are formed and clothed with substance according to our interpretation. These thoughts then express in the manifest world as "things." The universe was created by God through thought. We create in the same way.

It is quite a responsibility to know that our every thought creates!

Staying With It: (?)T + (?)A = E

Consider the above equation. T (thought) plus A (action) equals E (expression). But a variable has been added.

We have the ability to stretch our capacity to think in the same way that an athlete can increase his or her body's capability to withstand stress through practice and determination. We can interject a thought of greater intensity, or we can act in a more productive manner. We choose how much of our creative energies we are willing to invest in life. The equation, therefore, becomes relative because the variable of human will has been added.

If you are a bridge player, you may be aware that its forerunner was a game called *whist*. In the following poem we see the similarities in the parts played by thought and action in life and in the game of whist.

> *Life is a game of whist. From unseen*
> > *sources*
> *The cards are shuffled, and the hands are*
> > *dealt.*
> *Blind are our efforts to control the forces*
> *That, though unseen, are no less strongly*
> > *felt.*
>
> . . .
>
> *I do not like the way the cards are*
> > *shuffled,*
> *But still I like the game and want to play*
> *And through the long, long night will I*
> *Play what I get, until the break of day.*[9]

With faith we persevere. But do we have faith? We may conclude we do not if we seek faith in the emotional realm. Faith is not emotion. It is activity. We often feel strong emotions regarding things in which we have little faith. To determine where our faith really lies, we must not look to our emotions, but to our perseverances.

Dr. Thomas Cooper was a man of faith. During the reign of Elizabeth I, he edited a dictionary, adding to it thirty-three thousand words, along with other improvements. He spent eight years collecting material and preparing his edition. One day in a fit of anger his wife entered his study and burned every note.

Dr. Cooper returned home and asked who was responsible for the destruction of his work. His wife confessed, but pleaded she had done it for his good because she feared he would kill himself with overwork.

Dr. Cooper sighed patiently, then sat down to another eight years of collecting material!

The Creative Activity of Love

The old-fashioned word was *charity.* In the Revised Standard Version of the Bible, the word *love* is used instead. In Paul's first letter to the

Corinthians[10] are described the various spiritual gifts (expressions of creativity); the greatest is love.[11]

Certainly love is a part of the creative personality in ways beyond mere devotion to one's work. Love must be an integral part of a person's nature in order for one to reflect creatively in the outer world.

Let me share a love story. When Cheryl and Tom married, they had little in common except for a mutual physical attraction (as is often the case) that, Cheryl admitted, was not sufficient grounds on which to build a marriage. With no common interests, as the years passed they grew further apart. They and their four children lived together like boarders—separate individuals sleeping and eating under one roof, with no communication except criticism for one another.

Tom owned "his" own business and insisted that Cheryl work "for" him. She could not write checks on "his" checking account nor did she receive a salary for her work. They were "together" constantly, at home and at work, yet not together at all. They seemed bound by mutual needs—his, for an unpaid housekeeper/secretary; and hers, for financial security for herself and their children.

One day a serious argument erupted, a rare instance of their communication of honest feelings to each other. Had it been handled properly, this could have been constructive, but Tom concluded a list of unrealistic grievances thrown about by both parties by informing Cheryl that he was "sick of looking at her." Now it is little wonder that he was "sick of looking at her." With this constant "togetherness," Cheryl was surely "sick of looking at him" as well.

For Cheryl, however, it was as if all the hurts of past years culminated in this remark. She made no reply, but walked away, in effect shutting Tom completely out of her life. They continued to live in the same house and work together, but they were total strangers. Though Cheryl did not believe in divorce, she began seeking ways to become financially independent in order to free herself from what she felt to be an intolerable situation.

About this time Cheryl started attending a Unity church and was thrilled by its positive approach to life. Surely Tom would be as excited as she! He not only rejected her invitation to accompany her to a service, but was actively antagonized by this new interest and resentful of what he described as her "desertion" of her own church, of which they were nominal members.

As Cheryl and I talked, she expressed frustration that, having discovered the principles of practical Christianity, she was unable to put them to practice in the relationship closest to her—that which existed in her own family. We discussed her plans for divorce. With the insight Cheryl had gained, she understood that most of Tom's peculiarities were the results of deep-rooted childhood insecurities. She realized, too, that should she divorce Tom and remarry without changing her own inward self, she would likely find herself married to another "Tom," with the additional complications of ex-spouses and stepchildren with which to contend.

Through reading and attending classes, Cheryl learned that all things begin in the mind with thought. If this were true, she reasoned, then thought was the cause of this inharmonious relationship—thoughts innocent of their destructive quality, and not her thoughts alone, but damaging thoughts, nevertheless. The effect of these thoughts was proceeding in a predictable way, to the dissolution of her family.

As a thinking, creative human being, Cheryl recognized that she had the power to introduce a new and different kind of thought—a thought of love—into this relationship. If it found a corresponding thought within the consciousness of her husband or children, then the predicted effect would be altered.

Cheryl began looking for and affirming the good qualities in Tom and her children. She was surprised at the admirable attributes she rediscovered. She made an agreement with herself to abstain from dwelling on their shortcomings for a certain period of time. This was the most difficult part of her endeavor, for habit does not die easily. Finally, she took the important step of attempting to reestablish communication with her husband and children and to show them the love she was not even sure she still felt.

Tom was understandably skittish at first, but gradually he responded; and with effort on both sides, their marriage has become a happy one. Business has improved. Cheryl, realizing that she and Tom would have more to share if they were together less, insisted upon finding work elsewhere. She now is financially independent, but has no intention of leaving Tom who, to prove his sincerity, has added her name to "their" joint checking account. The six "boarders" who lived in a house have become a family, and this house is now a home.

This happy ending did not take place easily, or overnight, but over a period of time and as a result of much prayer, understanding, and determination. It began with one single thought of love. Cheryl expressed her creativity in the most beautiful of ways.

"It was worth it!" she told me.

Creative Characteristics

Since creative expression is an essential part of our lives, it is good to examine some of the qualities that make up the creative individual. A tool that may prove helpful in remembering these characteristics is found in the letters that spell the word *creativity*.

The "creative" individual possesses attributes of:

> C-aring
> R-enunciation
> E-valuation
> A-ffirmation
> T-enacity
> I-nitiative
> V-ision
> I-magination
> T-hanksgiving
> Y-outhfulness

1. *Caring:* Creativity is not measured only in the discovery of a technological breakthrough or the formulation of a theory that will bring about a quantum jump in human progress. Creativity is finding a way to soften a hard blow, to brighten a dark situation, or to solve a difficulty in a strained relationship. Begin by sincerely caring about what you do and loving those who benefit from it.

2. *Renunciation:* Renounce those attitudes which no longer play a beneficial role in your life. Free yourself of habit patterns that are not

conducive to your flow of creative expression. Deny negative concepts with such statements as: I refuse to react to appearances. I freely let go all thoughts less than Truth. I am no longer bound by the false belief that I am in any way limited.

3. *Evaluation:* Learn to discriminate and to set priorities. Often we fail to achieve our goals because we attempt too many things at one time. Eliminate unnecessary, time-consuming thoughts and activities.

   Be honest in evaluating your abilities. Most of us devaluate ourselves. There have been many accounts of what percentage of the human brain is actually used. For purposes of illustration, let us be overly generous and say that the average person utilizes 10 percent of the brain's capacity to operate. If we could use an additional 1 percent, our performance would be above average; if 2 percent, it would be superior. Should we stretch our ability to the point where we were using 15 percent of our brain power, no one would question our genius.

   Knowing this, you can safely set a goal,

raise it by 10 percent and still be underestimating your true potential.

4. *Affirmation:* When God created, He called all things "good."[12] Make firm in your consciousness that you are a child of God, His creation, which He called "very good."[13] Affirm: *I am a child of joy, a child of good. Through my creativity I express my love for everyone in the world. I feel like helping, I want to help, I have time to help. I will smile and be pleasant in my every word and action, as I joyfully and caringly put into practice God's creative ideas.*

5. *Tenacity:*   *Little drops of water,*
              Little grains of sand,
              Make the mighty ocean
              And the pleasant land. [14]

Remember that the person who succeeds is likely the one who, like the drops of water and grains of sand, keeps right on when things look gloomiest. This is the time to sharpen your efforts! History is filled with such successes. Had he quit at his first defeat, Abraham Lincoln would have been a one-term congressman!

6. *Initiative:* Take the first step! Once you decide what you want and prove that you are serious by getting started, the great creative Power in whose image we were formed furnishes ideas. When we open ourselves to the creative flow, it cooperates to the point of overflowing.

7. *Vision:* Vision is that which sees beyond appearances. Develop your inner vision by realizing your true capabilities. You are limited only by those limitations you place upon yourself. Emerson wrote:[15]

> The key to every man is his thought. . . . The life of man is a self-evolving circle which, from a ring imperceptibly small, rushes on all sides outwards to new and larger circles, and that without end. The extent to which this generation of circles . . . will go depends on the force or truth of the individual soul.

8. *Imagination:* You have within you a magic kingdom that you alone rule. In this kingdom, you have access to all that is needed for

happiness and success. Within this kingdom, you can create the blueprint for whatever you want in life.

This amazing faculty—imagination—is, however, a two-edged sword. Its function is to translate the formless into form; in this, you have a sacred trust. When exercised with love, imagination creates that which is beneficial to all. Uncontrolled, a hell is created where a heaven exists.

9. *Thanksgiving:* You can offer no higher prayer to God than that of praise. Since God experiences through us, there is no greater thanksgiving than our own feelings of joy. Personalize the words of the Psalmist: *This is the day which the Lord has made; let us rejoice and be glad in it!*[16]

10. *Youthfulness:* Jesus said that we must become as little children.[17] By this, he meant we must regain the "childlike" quality of expectancy, the feeling that there is nothing we cannot do or be.

Give up the old race belief that there is not enough time to accomplish your goals. To accept this is to accept premature defeat. You are never too old nor too young to begin. Your desires would not have been planted in your heart were they not intended to grow to fruition. The happy Truth is that you have all eternity to complete them.

Whether I come to my own today or in ten thousand or ten million years,
I can cheerfully take it now, or with equal cheerfulness I can wait. [18]

Chapter 9

Divine Discontent

⟋

> *"Blessed are those who mourn,*
> *for they shall be comforted."*[1]

> *Children, behold the Chimpanzee*
> *He sits on the ancestral tree*
> *From which we sprang in ages gone.*
> *I'm glad we sprang, had we held on*
> *We might, for aught that I can say,*
> *Be horrid Chimpanzees today.*[2]

This poem is quoted "tongue in cheek" for obvious reasons. First, the chimpanzee is not a "horrid" creature, but a beautiful and highly developed creation of God, expressing itself magnificently. Second, neither evolutionist nor non-evolutionist claims that man evolved *from* the chimpanzee.

There was a time, nevertheless, when man did not look or act precisely as does twenty-first-century man. He was smaller. His arms were proportionately longer, and he tended to slump forward as he walked. His body was covered with hair. His jaw and teeth were large and jutted outward. His forehead was lower. The sounds he made to communicate would be strange to our ears. Were we to meet this "man" walking down a street today, we would surely take a second look as we proceeded speedily on our way.

The point illustrated by this poem is that planted within this man, primitive though he appears by today's standards, there was a divine spark that pushed him onward to greater achievements. He had instincts just as animals have, but he had something more, something that would eventually overshadow instinct and separate him forever from the rest of the animal kingdom. He had a mind with unlimited potential.

When our son was born, his sister—three years his senior—could amuse herself for hours laughing uproariously at his funny gurglings and infantile attempts to coordinate muscles. Back and forth she ran, reporting to me his every new and, to her, hilarious antic. Within a few years, however, he was able to speak as clearly and walk as straight as she.

As we look back a million years or so at this fascinating ancestor of ours, we, too, may feel a sense of superiority. If so, we might remind ourselves of the small child's patronizing attitude toward a younger brother or sister who has not yet learned to speak or walk upright. The promise of greater accomplishment is there, just as it was with man in his infancy. We, his descendants, are the living proof of this fact.

On a hot day in July of 1969, the world watched in fascination as astronaut Neil Armstrong took the first step on the moon and described it as "one small step for a man, one giant leap for mankind."[3] This step was as nothing compared to the moment when a creature so many years ago felt the stirrings of discontent and suddenly realized that he had within himself a strange new power—the power to think and, by thinking, to alter his world.

This was humankind's greatest moment!

The Awakening

In the book of Genesis, we read the account of Adam and Eve. In the Garden of Eden their every need was provided for. They had no reason to create, to dream, to hope—even to think. The Garden of Eden has been pictured by theologians, politically motivated in early Christianity and perpetuated in modern times out of ignorance, superstition, and fear, as the ideal state from which man, by "original sin," fell.

How many of us would choose to return to such a state?

We have a poodle named Cream Puff. All her needs are met. She is fed. She is taken for walks and rides in the car. She is constantly petted, praised, and loved. All that is asked in return is that she be cute, obedient, and loving. These requirements she meets admirably.

From reading the first three chapters of Genesis, this appears similar to the condition in which Adam and Eve found themselves. This might be desirable for a nonthinker. The word *man,* however, comes from a word that means "to think."[4] Man, therefore, is a "thinker," and with that first independent thought, he was no longer content in the role of "nonthinker." This was surely consistent with God's plan, since He named man (defined his nature) and created him in His own image and after His likeness.[5]

My little Cream Puff is an ideal companion so long as I am in the mood to pet her and bask in her unquestioning adoration. There are times, however, when this is not totally satisfying. As a human being, I need companions to share my thoughts, to stimulate my mind, even to disagree with my opinions. Cream Puff does none of these. Only people satisfy these needs. Surely our need is but a reflection of our Father's need, and in creating man, it was His intent to create a being worthy of His companionship and capable of independent thought.

We read further in Genesis that "the serpent was more subtle than any other wild creature that the Lord God had made."[6] Now Adam and Eve represent not two people, but the masculine and feminine aspects of "generic man."[7] Naturally, it was Eve, the feeling nature, to whom the serpent made his first approach. It is always through our feeling nature that those subtle urgings of divine discontent first appear. The feeling nature inevitably presents her discontent to the thinking nature, just as Eve offered fruit to her husband.[8] By eating the fruit, by appropriating independent thought-action, man (male and female) forever relinquished his role as God's pet, loved and cared for only, and became even more—a child of God with responsibilities and unlimited potentialities.

In the allegory of the "fall of man," the serpent is invariably portrayed as the villain and Eve his foolish yet willing accomplice. Perhaps the serpent has been maligned and, rather than being the villain of our story, is in reality the catalyst, that spark of divine discontent which drove man from his state of dreamlike bliss into a world of creative expression.

Yet we read that "The Lord God said to the serpent . . . cursed are you . . . ."[9] According to *Mysteries of Genesis*, "the curse was not imposed directly by Jehovah but as a result of man's breaking certain laws."[10] It is easy to call these stirrings of discontent "cursed," for they are, indeed, unsettling to the feeling nature. ("I will put enmity between you and the woman."[11]) Our goal, like that of Moses,[12] is to lift up the serpent of divine discontent in the wilderness of our consciousness and heed the voice of our highest calling. Then, instead of the "fall of man," this allegory in our own life becomes "the awakening of man."

Too long we have been taught to feel contempt and shame for these allegorical ancestors who yielded to temptation. Instead, we should feel a surge of love and pride for those predecessors who so long ago took that first giant leap of independent thought.

> *A shape waked up from eating herb and*
>   *grain.*
> *It chanced to see the stars, and with that*
>   *look*
> *Came wonderment, and Longing in its*
>   *train.*
> *The food untasted lay. A beating pain*
> *Smote at its forehead, but it waked again*
> *And yet again. And it thought.*
> *Lo! Man stood upright as the stars did*
>   *wane!*[13]

"Blessed Are Those Who Mourn"

One of Jesus' most provocative statements is, "Blessed are those who mourn for they shall be comforted."[14]

The literalist's belief is that we are blessed when we experience tragedy, for we do not receive our reward or punishment on Earth, but in heaven or hell. Thus, the more pain we endure, the greater our recompense after death. This concept is appalling to those who study Truth. Still we wonder what it is that Jesus is actually saying to us.

What is there about mourning that can be termed *blessed*? As we understand the word, nothing could be less blessed. Mournfulness is an attitude that makes not only the mourner miserable, but everyone else as well. We have all known people who carry their woes about like prizes to be shared, and we avoid them as if they had the plague (which, in a metaphysical sense, they do).

The traditional interpretation of this teaching is not consistent with the New Testament image of Jesus—the man who attended wedding feasts, evidenced quick wit and a ready sense of humor, ate with publicans and sinners, and loved little children. In Jesus, we do not find a man of sorrows, but a man of joy! We must, therefore, look at this saying from a different standpoint.

Throughout Jesus' ministry it was his custom to tell stories and teach through precepts that whet the curiosity of his listeners, forcing them to look beyond the surface to deeper and more meaningful truths. Surely this was his intent when he spoke these paradoxical words.

Perhaps the mourning of which Jesus spoke could be called divine discontent. We human beings experience strange yearnings akin to mourning during periods of growth and change in consciousness. Without this inner mourning or discontent, our lives would become static and barren. We are indeed blessed when we "mourn," for we then have the opportunity to fulfill the inborn urge to move upward, to strive for greater attitudes of being, to accomplish higher goals. We then know that God has a new and larger assignment for us, and we rejoice as we wait with expectation to discover what this assignment might be.

Dissatisfaction Vs. Divine Discontent

To successfully carry out our new commission, it is imperative that we recognize the difference between divine discontent and simple dissatisfaction. One way to determine this is by understanding some of the attitudes that characterize each one.

Everyone experiences times of dissatisfaction. This is natural. These periods may come frequently, but are usually of short duration. We generally think of dissatisfaction as pertaining to relatively minor things. These may be easily corrected by changing our thought patterns. Dissatisfaction may occur when we feel we are not receiving sufficient appreciation for what we do. Sometimes an outer condition may need adjustment. We may not care for a particular job, yet not feel the need to make a total change in lifestyle. Our dissatisfaction may be corrected by simply doing the same work for a different company.

Divine discontent, on the other hand, has its root in the inner consciousness. Divine discontent is not the impulsiveness that causes one to rush into a venture with little thought and no preparation. It can be distinguished from impetuosity in several ways. First, its stirrings do not come about suddenly, nor do they diminish quickly; rather, they feel "even more right" as time passes. Second, its primary thrust is not self-glorification. Divine discontent, carried out, brings good to everyone concerned. Third, a way is always provided to achieve the fulfillment of these yearnings, for they are God desiring through us.

Let me share the experience of two acquaintances.

Andrew attended a church service and was immediately convinced that God's voice had spoken to him, instructing that he become a great minister in the Truth movement. That very day he applied for entrance into ministerial school. Andrew had no source of income, but he did have a plan. He proposed to divorce his wife so she might collect welfare funds to support them and their children, while Andrew—legally abandoning the family—attended school. This, he explained, was God's way of providing their prosperity. He and his wife would then be remarried after his ordination.

It came as a shock to Andrew that his plan

and lofty recommendation were received by the school officials with something less than enthusiasm. He was kindly advised to return home, settle his financial problems, work in the church, attend classes, and then determine how he felt about the ministry. This he did not do. In a few weeks, Andrew was engrossed in a new and equally unrealistic project. Andrew was indeed discontent, but his direction was far from divine.

Amy had much the same initial reaction to the impact of the Truth message. Rather than making an abrupt decision to enter the ministry, however, she decided to wait and see if her feelings passed the test of time. Meanwhile, she studied and became a teacher in her church. Convinced that her desire was a lasting one, for her highest good and that of everyone else, she applied for ministerial school, was accepted, and is now successfully serving as minister of her first church.

We are indeed blessed when we "mourn" if we are experiencing the growth pains of divine discontent. Oscar Wilde said, "Discontent is the first step in the progress of a man or a nation." [15] Longfellow wrote, "Our pleasures and our discontents are rounds by which we may ascend."[16] Francis Quarles expressed it this way: "Be always displeased at what thou art, if thou desire to attain to what thou art not; for where thou has pleased thyself, there thou abidest."[17]

Blessed are those who experience divine discontent, for they shall find the comfort of life's ever-expanding goodness.

When God Nudges, Move!

As impulsiveness and divine discontent are incompatible, so are procrastination and divine discontent.

Beverly and David had been active members of a particular denomination for many years, as had their families before them. Their children attended Sunday school. Beverly was president of the women's group. David was a member of the church board and the teacher of an adult Sunday school class.

The situation was comfortable. It required little thought or action, yet Beverly and David were not totally satisfied. For some time Beverly had been reading Unity literature. She discussed these new ideas with David, who was intrigued by them and eager to learn more. Subtly, he fed his Sunday school class the Truth message, carefully veiled in traditional terminology.

Suddenly, a dynamic Unity church was organized in their area. David suggested that they make a change for their own growth and that of their children. Beverly, however, hesitated, claiming that even though they were not learning where they were, they were growing by sharing their knowledge with others; David, through his teaching and she, through her work with the women.

The church they attended had long been a troubled one. Disagreements again erupted and there were strong differences of opinion. David, being a forceful individual with the capacity to lead others, was apparently considered a threat by some of his fellow board members. Those who disagreed with David realized they had no way to control his influence . . . except through Beverly. A special meeting was called and the minority present decided that Beverly be asked to resign as president of the women's group and that a professional coordinator be hired to replace her.

Beverly was deeply hurt and bitter at what

she considered unjust and un-Christian action. But as a result she, David, and their children immediately began their active work in Unity. Soon both Beverly and David were able to say without qualification that what occurred had been the best thing that ever happened to them. David is again teaching, but it is no longer necessary that he veil his words for fear of criticism.

Beverly later faced a physical challenge that she felt would have been much more serious had it not been for her understanding of Truth principles and the prayers and personal contact of like-minded people. "Had I been willing to act when David first suggested it, we would have avoided much unhappiness," she told me. "One lesson I learned is that when God gives you a nudge, you'd better do something, or He'll give you a shove!"

Emerson wrote, "The man or woman who would have remained a sunny garden-flower with no room for its roots and too much sunshine for its head, by the falling of the walls and the neglect of the gardener is made the banian of the forest, yielding shade and fruit to wide neighborhoods of men."[18]

Hell

The story is told of a bride who discovered on her honeymoon that her husband did not believe in hell. The distraught young woman placed a long-distance telephone call to her mother. "Oh, Mother," she cried pathetically, "Harold is an atheist. He doesn't even believe in hell!"

"Don't worry, dear," the mother reassured her. "Between the two of us, we'll show him how wrong he is!"

Unfortunately, many people are much like this bride in their religious beliefs. They equate the necessity for a belief in hell with faith in God. In Unity, we recognize that God and the traditional concept of hell are totally inconsistent with each other.

When I was a child, one of the hymns we sang in church was "Almost Persuaded,"[19] composed, ironically, by a man named Bliss. It began on the hopeful note,

> *Almost persuaded, now to believe,*
> *Almost persuaded; Christ to receive.*

but ended despairingly,

Almost cannot avail; Almost is but
    to fail.
Sad, sad, that bitter wail, Almost,
    but lost!

While this would hardly qualify as a "joy song," it does contain a message—that of the tragic loss of potential. If there were a hell, it would surely be the knowledge of what we could have been, what we could have done, but did not, because we refused to follow those divine stirrings.

Theodore Roosevelt in a speech in 1899 said, "Far better it is to dare mighty things, to win glorious triumphs, even though checkered by failure, than to take rank with those poor spirits who neither enjoy much nor suffer much because they live in the gray twilight that knows not victory nor defeat."[20]

William Gilmore Simms, a southern novelist and historian prior to the Civil War, left these words: "Better that we should err in action than wholly refuse to perform. The storm is so much better than the calm, as it declares the presence of a living principle. Stagnation is something worse than death. It is corruption also."[21]

There may be those who fail to take action for fear of eternal damnation. The beauty of the Unity viewpoint is that, unlike the flames in which some fear they will burn forever, hell is the symbol of the purifying fire that consumes only that which is not compatible to the true Christ nature in us. Charles Fillmore wrote: "Hell . . . represents a corrective state of mind. When error has reached its limit, the retroactive law asserts itself, and judgment, being part of that law, brings the penalty upon the transgressor. This penalty is not punishment, but discipline."[22]

The "hell" referred to in the Bible as "Gehenna" was a place outside Jerusalem where the city's waste was burned.[23] In this same way, we are symbolically purified, then offered limitless opportunities for growth through our continued divine discontent.

Benjamin Franklin wrote: "Were the offer made true, I would engage to run again from beginning to end, the same career of life. All I would ask should be the privilege of the author to correct, in a second edition, certain errors of the first."[24]

And this is precisely what each of us is given

every day—"the privilege to correct, in another edition, certain errors of the first."

Spirals

Where are we going? What does God have in mind for the human race? Perhaps humankind is only now entering its generic adolescence, mature enough to seek independence, yet not mature enough to know exactly what to do with it.

Each person in his or her lifetime passes through all stages the race of humankind has experienced. It follows that with each thought which lifts us above the ordinary, we lift not only ourselves, but our brother and sister as well. Jesus explained it this way, "And I, when I am lifted up from the earth, will draw all men to myself."[25]

It was discontent that invented the wheel, the automobile, the airplane, the spacecraft—as expressions of the divine idea of freedom. It was discontent that brought into being art, music, dancing—as expressions of the divine idea of joy. It was discontent that opened the way for the genius of Einstein, the philosophical understanding of Plato, the scientific advancements of Pasteur, the religious trailblazing of Myrtle and Charles Fillmore—as expressions of the divine idea of intelligence. It is discontent that pours forth in friendship and kindness, in forgiveness, in one man's lending a helping hand to another in need, in prayers offered twenty-four hours a day in our Silent Unity Telephone Prayer Ministry—as expressions of the divine idea of love.

We live not in one world, but in two. We live in the world of appearance, where good may or may not be seen; yet simultaneously, in the world of Spirit, at the center of our being, where, when we look with our inward eye, there is only absolute goodness. Perhaps our goal is to blend these two worlds, as did Jesus, till the inner and the outer are one.

The Psalmist wrote:

> *What is man that thou art mindful*
> *of him,*
> *and the son of man that thou dost*
> *care for him?*
> *Yet thou has made him little less*
> *than God,*
> *and dost crown him with glory*
> *and honor.*[26]

Where will these stirrings of divine discontent take us? Is there a limit? Who of us can imagine?

———————◄o►———————

Discontent Directors

1. Do not be unduly disturbed by feelings of discontent. Dissatisfaction passes. Divine discontent is a gift of God, an expression of God's law of love. Divine discontent will never be the incentive for anything foolish or harmful for you or anyone else. It is the movement of Spirit within you toward goodness and growth. Divine discontent might be compared to the feelings a student experiences when nearing the school's commencement day. There may be a sense of sadness, for change is imminent. Know, however, that something even better is now approaching.

2. Affirm that you have the ability to carry out your new assignment. Say: *I am a radiant, glowing spark of light with limitless possibilities. God has graduated me because I have completed my course and am ready for a new assignment.*

Deny any appearances to the contrary. Declare: "I have no doubts as to my capabilities. If God trusts me, who am I to question His judgment? There is nothing that the Father and I together cannot accomplish!"

3. Test your feelings. Do not act impulsively or postpone too long that which must be done. There is a right time and place for action. Your way will be made clear.

4. Give thanks for these stirrings of discontent. They are God's way of showing His confidence in you. They are, in effect, a "celestial pat on the back."

TRANSCENDENCIES

Chapter 10

Free Will

⌒⎯⎯⎯⎯⎯⎯⎯⎯⎯⎯⎯⎯⎯⌒

"Then God said, ' . . . let them have dominion.'" [1]

Playwright Oscar Wilde arrived at his club following the first production of a play that had proved less than successful. Excitedly, a friend rushed to him. "How did your play go, Oscar?" he asked.

"The play was magnificent!" was Wilde's haughty response. "The audience, unfortunately, was a failure."

This incident illustrates something more important than Wilde's lack of humility. Rather than accepting the verdict of his audience—verbally admitting it, thus giving it additional power, then acting the role of failure—Wilde chose how he would think, chose his words, and chose his future as well.

It was not within his power to alter the audience reaction to his play, but he could and did affect his thoughts and words regarding their reaction.

Charles Fillmore wrote: "The will is the man. . . . We know that God is the Great Unlimited, and man, His 'image' and 'likeness,' must be of the same character; consequently man has the same freedom that God has to act in the fulfillment of desire."[2]

Reaction Vs. Free Will

The destiny of us human beings lies in our capacity to choose. This realization is the primary characteristic distinguishing us from the animal kingdom. Yet not everyone recognizes and exercises this ability. We might visualize a beautiful apple tree, weighted down with ripe, red apples. All we need do is pluck and eat them. But if we are blind and no one has told us of such a tree, as far as we are concerned it is not there.

So it is with free will. If we are spiritually blind, as far as we are concerned it does not exist. It is available to all, but like every gift it must be accepted and used.

Too many people are tossed about by the winds of cause and effect—causes not consciously set in motion and effects in which they are powerless participants. Cause and effect is the most elementary expression of the law, and we can rise above it by interjecting a higher expression of God's law of love—our power to choose the way we think and feel. We determine future effects by choosing our causes.

Recognition of free will appears a recent development. A dog, cat, or other animal may show preference for one person or reject a brand of pet food in favor of another. Nevertheless, these are relatively unconscious choices, reactions based on sense perception as opposed to reason. This does not give us cause to look down on our animal friends, for the majority of human decisions are made in this same way. The difference is that humans alone have the capacity to *consciously* choose what we will think and feel.

To have free will, however, does not imply

that we possess the power to choose our every experience (though it might be that in not choosing, our choice is unconsciously made). What we do have is the right to choose how we will *think* regarding our experiences; then as we choose our thoughts, our feelings automatically follow.

Two people may undergo experiences generally regarded as traumatic. To one, it may seem devastating. The other may pass through it with no concern. The difference is in their conscious or unconscious choice of thought.

Parents should always be aware of their responsibility in this regard. Most children do not recognize their ability to choose their thoughts and feelings and are influenced by the parents' reactions. If we speak words of fear or allow our children to sense our uneasiness, they are likely to react and be affected, not by the situation, but by their thoughts and feelings about it.

I know two brothers, now in their middle years, who are terrified of storms. As children, their mother hid with them under the bed each time it rained. Today they recognize that society would frown on grown men huddling beneath office furniture, yet they repeatedly call each other on the telephone at the first sign of a dark cloud, receiving some sense of security by being together in this way in case of storm.

If we refuse to impress our children's minds with our own prejudices and fears, they will emerge unharmed and better for having had the experiences from which we, their parents, would like to protect them. Progress, for society and the individual, rarely comes without growing pains.

As the Bible is an allegory showing the growth of man from his infancy to the recognition of his Christhood, we find in the twelve sons of Jacob, who became the twelve tribes of Israel, the representation of the rudimentary phases of natural man's faculties of consciousness. Among them the faculty of will is absent.[3] Not until Jesus called together his twelve disciples, symbolizing the refined or spiritualized faculties in man, does "will" appear, represented by the disciple Matthew.[4] Metaphysically, this would indicate that the awareness of free will occurs only after we have gained the maturity to recognize and follow the indwelling Christ.

Will in humans is the executive faculty that carries out what we decree. All thoughts and feelings entering or leaving our consciousness are judged and, if deemed worthy to proceed as words and actions, passed to the executive office of will, where they are carried out by the "Matthew" in us. The name *Matthew* in Hebrew means "gift of Jehovah,"[5] so we see that free will in humanity is truly a gift to be accepted or rejected.

> *Decide not rashly. The decision made*
> *Can never be recalled. The gods implore*
> > *not,*
> *Plead not, solicit not; they only offer*
> *Choice and occasion, which once being*
> > *passed*
> *Return no more. Dost thou accept*
> > *the gift?*[6]

Choose This Day

When Millie was a child, she was diagnosed as having contracted scarlet fever and whooping cough. Before she recovered, she was struck by a trolley car. As a result, her vision and hearing were lost. Her parents attempted everything they knew to effect a cure, with no success. During this time, Millie became proficient at using the hand alphabet and reading braille.

The years passed and all Millie's family were gone, leaving her alone. When she was about age fifty, someone took her to a hospital for what he said would be a blood test. It was a state mental hospital where she remained for more than nineteen years. Never during that time was her hearing tested nor did anyone pay attention to what she tried to tell them. Eventually, she gave up attempting communication, and in addition to being blind and deaf, was considered mute and mentally ill. Her food was regularly stolen, and she was in constant danger of attack by other residents. Millie retained her sanity by reading her braille Bible and inspirational magazines.

When an instructor for the vision- and hearing-impaired visited the hospital to determine if there were any deaf patients, the authorities stated they knew of none. The instructor took their word and left.

One day a deaf volunteer, noting Millie's dignity, became suspicious that her only problems might be the inability to see and hear. He reached for her hand and with manual letters spelled out "H-I." Millie grabbed his hand and excitedly spelled back, "What's happening in the world?" Eventually, the volunteer won Millie's release from the hospital.

At the age of seventy-one, after two years of freedom, Millie became a college student and a sought-after lecturer. She would "hear" with the help of a portable Tele-touch, a machine similar to a typewriter with a button on the back. Letters punched on the keyboard were translated into the raised dots of braille on the button.

After Millie made an "A" on a college theme, she wrote: "My good friends, do not let life pass you by. The art of life can consist of the ability of seeing the beauty of one's life. . . . For without beauty, life is a dead end."

Millie had been treated as if she were insane. Others, deaf like her, had accepted insanity. Millie used her free will to select what she would think and be. She chose sanity and hope and was rewarded with a happy, productive life.[7]

Joshua, after leading the Hebrew people into the Promised Land, admonished them, "Choose this day whom you will serve . . . but as for me and my house, we will serve the Lord."[8]

We, too, must choose whom we will serve: health or illness, prosperity or poverty, love or inharmony, success or failure. No one wants to really suffer, but some seem willing to suffer just a little to gain sympathy and attention.

A little is too much. A little is like the yeast that expands the bread. A little is like the seed that grows into a towering tree. There is no room in our house—in our consciousness—for even a little area of darkness. We must choose God (good) with no reservations, if we are to be truly free.

The Power in Disagreeing

Two men sat side by side on a bus. One noted that the other was reading Unity literature. "I see you're a metaphysician," he observed.

"That's right," the other replied.

"Then would you mind trading seats with me?" the first man requested. "I'm sitting in a draft!"

I recently found myself in much the same predicament. Having volunteered to work at the headquarters of a friend who was a candidate for the city council, I unthinkingly selected a chair in front of an air-conditioning unit. After battling billowing papers for some time, I explained to the volunteer next to me that I was moving to the other room to escape the breeze. "I don't blame you," she replied with genuine concern. "I *do* hope you don't catch cold!"

Catch cold . . . ? I mused. Why should I catch cold? After a moment I realized what she meant. Until then I had not recognized how well my subconscious mind had assimilated the truths faithfully fed it for so long. Nevertheless, having been reminded of that deeply ingrained superstition, I decided to verbally reaffirm the Truth of my good health. "I'm sure I won't!" I told my friend. Needless to say, I did not catch cold.

We, as Truth students, must not only know the Truth, but be alert to situations where we are exposed to false beliefs. At another friend's home, I observed her dutifully warning her small son not to get his feet wet because he was inclined to catch cold. With the best of intentions, this loving and well-meaning mother had committed two serious errors: First, she reinforced in the child's mind the false belief that he catches cold easily; and second, she passed on the misinformation that by getting his feet wet, colds would occur.

Reason shows no logic in such a concept. Surely the child bathes. Does he catch cold each time, or is the water that runs from the faucet into the tub less harmful than that which falls from the sky? Or perhaps Mother has devised a method by which the boy can bathe while protecting those vulnerable feet.

My friend is not one with whom I could debate the issue without reinforcing it in her mind. Still I can "know" the Truth for them. In this case, I mentally denied the boy's cold proneness, while affirming his good health.

Many other views are equally primitive. Each time we hear such stories, we might do well to conjure up in our imagination the picture of a witch doctor chanting and dancing, as a reminder to guard our thoughts.

After treatment for a minor physical complaint, my friend Joanna asked her physician what brought about the condition. "Birthdays!" was the prompt reply. "My first inclination was to ask why Aquarians were more predispositioned toward this ailment than others," Joanna laughingly told me. "Then it dawned on me what the doctor meant. Age! That old bugaboo! It's a cop-out for everything! It was easy to reject the diagnosis. I wasn't even twenty the first time I experienced this disorder!"

The medical profession is not alone in perpetuating misinformation. The child begins life with his parents as his sole authority figures. Gradually, others are added. From them, he is offered a smorgasbord of fact and fantasy. In the natural order of things, these figures are gradually discarded, but the subconscious mind retains the information with which it is programmed, for good or ill. The individual is not finished with authority figures. A whole new set emerges— the doctor, the professor, the television commentator, the printed word, and especially the peer group.

This poem illustrates the way many people unquestioningly follow these self-appointed authorities:

The statesman throws his shoulders back
and straightens out his tie,

And says, "My friends, unless it rains,
*   the weather will be dry."*
And when this thought into our brains
*   has percolated through,*
We common people nod our heads and
*   loudly cry, "How true!"*[9]

It is our job to recognize ourselves as "un-common people" and to loudly cry, "How false!" each time we hear lies foisted off as reality. We must, if we are to control our life, learn to distinguish fact from opinion and to recognize that our opinions are as valid as anyone else's.

Words Unspoken and Spoken

At the College of Veterinary Medicine at Texas A & M University, treatment was given to pets diagnosed as having cancer. They were treated with the traditional methods used on human beings, including radiology and cobalt therapy. The director of the radiology section at the college reported that side effects are minimal. "Dogs don't have psychosomatic side effects. You see, dogs don't tell other dogs they're going to get sick or lose their hair from radiation."[10]

Human beings, however, are able to speak and communicate concepts. Through our words, we are able to bring life or its absence in both the qualitative and quantitative sense.

We read in the Gospel According to John that the world was formed through the Word.[11] The prophet Isaiah wrote, "So shall my word be that goes forth from my mouth; it shall not return to me empty, but it shall accomplish that which I purpose, and prosper in the thing for which I sent it."[12]

Charles Fillmore explained how our words take form:

> The spoken word carries vibrations through the universal ether, and also moves the intelligence inherent in every form, animate or inanimate. . . . Man, being the highest emanation of Divine Mind, has great directive power and is really co-operator with God in forming the universe . . .

The power of the word is given man to use. The better he understands the character of God and his own relation to humanity, the more unselfishly will he exercise this power. Some are using it in selfish ways, but this should not deter others who have a better understanding of the law from using it in righteous ways. . . . If we need things and if they are necessary to our happiness, it is not sacrilegious to set into action this higher law in attaining them. . . . The word of one in authority carries weight and produces far-reaching effects. . . .

If your word is selfish, that which will come to you through its use will be unsatisfactory . . . learn to speak words of righteousness only.[13]

We have free will in choosing our words. That we are now aware of the consequences of our words places on us a greater, but wonderful responsibility to choose wisely.

Ella Wheeler Wilcox wrote:

Talk happiness. The world is sad enough
Without your woe. No path is wholly
   rough.

   . . .

Talk faith. The world is better off without
Your uttered ignorance and morbid
   doubt.

   . . .

Talk health. The dreary, never-ending
   tale
Of mortal maladies is more than stale:
You cannot charm or interest or please
By harping on that minor chord, disease.
Say you are well, or all is well with you,
And God shall hear your words, and
   make them true.[14]

"Have a Good Life"

Comedian Red Skelton, no stranger to challenges, passed through our city. At the airport, he was directed to a celebrity lounge for privacy as he waited between flights. Almost immediately he was recognized, and soon reporters, photographers, and a crowd of fans were grouped about him, snapping pictures, asking questions, and seeking autographs.

Skelton was on his way to speak at a college where one of his topics would be religion. "People today are looking for God," he said. "During a recent question-and-answer session, a student asked me why he can't find God. I told him he can't find God the same way a thief can't find a policeman. He's not looking for Him." Skelton then suggested that the students "every morning write the word *Good* on a blackboard, then go out and do something for someone, expecting and getting nothing in return. Nothing is zero, so when you get home, scratch a zero out of your word and you will find 'God.'"

As he was leaving a man shook Skelton's hand and said, "Have a good morning, sir." Skelton glanced at his watch and noting it was almost noon, replied: "It's too late for that. Have a good life!"[15]

And that is exactly what we have the free will to do—have a good life! The circumstances of our life do not determine its quality. The fact that we have aspirations to rise above circumstance is proof that we have the ability to carry them out.

Thirty-one-year-old Annette is an example of one who uses her free will to "have a good life." Annette will soon receive her bachelor's degree, thirteen years after she enrolled in college. Many people older than she return to school, and many, working full time or raising families, take more years to finish.

What makes Annette unique is that she began college with only discouragements. She attended all of her classes in a wheelchair and will receive her diploma seated in that same wheelchair.

Annette's doctors attempted to dissuade her from so ambitious an undertaking as college, but Annette, who at age nine had been diagnosed as having muscular dystrophy, refused to "just sit back and become a vegetable."

"My peer group is no longer here," she said, referring to the children who received similar diagnoses at the same time as she. Then Annette spoke the key words, "I think some of them just gave up."

Annette did not give up. She used her free will to select a goal, to insist that she would accomplish it, and to fulfill the necessary requirements for the completion of that goal.

Annette is not through. Following graduation, Annette plans to attend graduate school, then become a teacher.[16]

On the physical plane, it is essential that we take action. We work from the center to the circumference of our mind, but once ideas reach the circumference, it is essential that we act. If we were intended only as thinkers, these marvelous bodies would be unnecessary; nor would we need the executive capacity to bring our "Word" into being.

In Job, we read, "You will decide on a matter, and it will be established for you, and light will shine on your ways."[17] Francis Cardinal Spellman said, "Pray as if everything depended on God, and work as if everything depended upon man."[18]

William James added: "No matter how full a reservoir of maxims one may possess, and no matter how good one's sentiments may be, if one has not taken advantage of every concrete opportunity to act, one's character may remain entirely unaffected for the better. With mere good intentions, hell is proverbially paved."[19]

Alarm Clocks

I read a newspaper article by a woman told by physicians that she was terminally ill. Jo's first question was, "Why me?" As she settled down to "acceptance," she came to the conclusion that there were four possible answers to her question.

First, God had selected this illness to punish her for her sins. Second, it was the result of "postmodern paranoia," a consequence of our tense and pressured society: pollution was contaminating the environment, thus poisoning us all. The third possibility she called, "pseudopsychological": life was so unbearable that she was unconsciously driven to seek death as an escape. The fourth alternative was her philosophy of existentialism: the universe is absurd; tragedies befall us as a matter of luck and occur randomly. This one just happened to "catch" her.

Jo's choice was her existentialist view—it had "just happened to her." This was the only explanation with which she felt she could happily live out her remaining days.[20]

But did these have to be her "remaining" days? As metaphysicians, we would reject all four explanations. Regarding Jo's fatalistic acceptance, we know that whatever occurs can be changed. It is not necessary or desirable to go over the past to determine the reason for the happening. When Jesus healed, he rarely concerned himself with the cause of disease. He simply freed the sufferer of the affliction.

We must never place a limitation on God's gift of life. I recall two women who were diagnosed by physicians as having incurable and short-term illnesses. Both were young and had small children. Both prayed selflessly and with sincerity that they be allowed to live—long enough to raise their children.

In both cases, after the youngest child left home, years after they were pronounced "cured" by physicians, the illnesses recurred; within a short time the women were dead. They—not God—fulfilled the bargain. With the great faith they had demonstrated, they could as easily have claimed and received "a long and healthful life, free of all appearance of disease."

But they did not. Both were devout Christians, but their "God" brought this disease on them for some mystical purpose beyond human understanding, and as an act of "grace," granted them a reprieve to perform their maternal duties.

And for this they praised Him.

In both cases, they set their own alarm clocks. But they set them much too early.

The Revealing Word says: "According to modern science this whole universe of forms can be dissolved into energy, from which it may again be formed. Science does not say that the directive and formative power is man, but the Bible so teaches and especially Jesus."[21]

We may not have conscious control over all outer circumstances of life. We do, however, have conscious control over our thoughts, words, and actions regarding these events. When we choose to change the inner through an act of free will, a miracle occurs.

The outer changes as well.

————◀○▶————

Will Executors

1. An oriental proverb states that we cannot prevent the birds from flying overhead, but

we need not let them nest in our hair. Be careful what you accept in consciousness. That which your mind is turned toward becomes a prayer, whether intentional or unintentional.

2. What you express verbally receives added power. Speak only what is good and true. Avoid words that tear down. Affirm the Truth of your being; deny the false. While you may not control every thought that flits through your mind, you can control your words. Set a guard at the gate of your mouth. Literally bite your tongue, if necessary.

3. You can control your actions. Remember that no one can "make you" think, feel, say, or do anything against your will. You are a free agent.

4. See yourself as a composition depicting your thoughts, words, and actions. You cannot blame fate, karma, environment, or heredity for your situation. While there may be outer influences, they are only that—influences. You alone choose your lot in life.

5. Exercise your free will. Like all good muscles, it develops with use.

Chapter 11

Grace

"Be transformed by the renewal of your mind."[1]

In the Old Testament book of Daniel is the story of the Babylonian King Nebuchadnezzar who made an image of gold and commanded all the people to bow down and worship it.[2] Those who refused were thrown into the fiery furnace. Three Jews, Shadrach, Meshach, and Abednego, were accused of violating this ordinance. Nebuchadnezzar was furious at their disobedience. Because of his esteem for their friend Daniel, however, he offered another opportunity, warning that if they again refused to worship the image, they would be burned in the furnace.

Shadrach, Meshach, and Abednego answered the king, "If it be so, our God whom we serve is able to deliver us."[3] In a fury, Nebuchadnezzar had the furnace heated seven times its regular temperature and the three men were bound, seized, and thrown into it.

When Nebuchadnezzar looked into the furnace, he saw Shadrach, Meshach, and Abednego walking unbound and unharmed, accompanied by a fourth man, described by the king as "like a son of the gods."[4] Nebuchadnezzar advanced to the door of the furnace and called Shadrach, Meshach, and Abednego to come forth. Seeing that they were untouched by the flames, he praised their God, proclaiming that the "Most High God"[5] had sent an angel to protect them. As a result, Shadrach, Meshach, and Abednego received great honors, and Nebuchadnezzar decreed that henceforth no disrespectful word could be uttered against Jehovah, their God.

Our Protecting Angel

The names of these three were changed from their original Hebrew to Babylonian after the conquest of the Jewish people. According to the *Metaphysical Bible Dictionary,* the name *Shadrach* refers to meekness as power acquired through true understanding. His original name, Hananiah, in Hebrew signifies "knowledge of Jehovah, the indwelling Christ, as love, mercy, goodness, and the channel of all power."[6] Thus, the meekness here indicated is the opposite of that misunderstood to be weakness. It is the strength that enables its possessor to fulfill the promise of Jesus that "the meek shall inherit the earth."[7]

The name *Meshach* denotes love.[8] His Hebrew name, Mishael, means "love, Godlikeness."[9] From this, we see the idea of a love transcending the human to achieve the quality of Godliness.

The name *Abednego* means light, understanding. He was renamed for the Babylonian and Assyrian deity Nego or Nebo, who was worshiped as the god of wisdom.[10] His Hebrew name, Azariah, alludes to "that in man which realizes Jehovah as a very present and efficient deliverer and help at all times."[11] In Abednego, we find the quality of wisdom gained through a realization of God as a personal, all-pervading, and indwelling Presence.

A king stands for activities of the will. "Nebuchadnezzar represents in us the human will backing itself up by the human intellect."[12] In the name *Nebuchadnezzar*, we again find a form of the name *Nebo*. Nebuchadnezzar, however, depicts a different type of wisdom than Abednego. He signifies wisdom turned toward things of the world, rather than toward the indwelling Lord.

The "golden image" built by Nebuchadnezzar symbolizes "mammon," those things which misrepresent themselves as real, as opposed to that which the enlightened inner Self knows to be true and enduring. The "fiery furnace" into which Shadrach, Meshach, and Abednego were cast is the testing that proves whether one will follow God or mammon. The fourth man in the furnace, described by the king as "like a son of the gods," is the consciousness of one's I AM in its spiritual unity with God.

This is one of the Old Testament's most fascinating stories, known to young and old alike. Sunday school children are as familiar with Shadrach, Meshach, and Abednego as are Bible scholars. It has a meaning for us, however, beyond that of an interesting tale about three men who were tossed into the fire, managed to survive, and were rewarded for their trust in God.

Metaphysically, we interpret these individuals and objects as aspects within the consciousness of the individual. Within each of us is a Shadrach, a Meshach, and an Abednego waiting to be called forth. Often they are in conflict with our Nebuchadnezzar, the dominant will, which likes to bow down to golden images of myriad form. When we develop those qualities of meekness, love, and wisdom and accept them as the Truth of our Being, we too are delivered from every fiery furnace we encounter. Even the Nebuchadnezzar within us is impressed and praises our God.

This realization is grace. The angel, the fourth man in the furnace, might be considered the personification of grace. When we fully recognize that we are always protected, regardless of appearances to the contrary, that God dwells in us as love and wisdom and expresses as personal guidance and protection, then we are living under the law of grace and our "protecting angel" is ever with us.

What Is Grace?

Grace is perhaps the most misunderstood theological philosophy. The confusion regarding its meaning is a result of accumulated misdefinitions.

Many people equate grace with the vicarious atonement. But grace is not the primitive belief that teaches that God required sacrifices and that Jesus, out of love for unworthy humanity, offered himself to be crucified to appease this gruesome god and put an end to his tyrannical tendencies toward violence. (This also ended "God's" lust for animal sacrifice, according to proponents of this theory.)

To accept such a concept is to "take the name of the Lord your God in vain."[13] This is not now and never was God's nature, but rather our misinterpretation of God. A friend once told me in all seriousness that the reason the God of the Old Testament and the God of the New Testament were so different is that God had learned about love from Jesus. Obviously, this is untrue. God is unchanging. It was the human's understanding of God's nature that changed, greatly assisted by Jesus' example.

Some groups teach that grace is "taking the name of Jesus," thus obtaining eternal salvation. Grace is not bestowed as a result of belief professed or ritual performed. Nor is grace a yielding of our free will to an overbearing despot, who requires that we act in a puppetlike fashion, incapable of independent thought or action, but prone toward peculiar words and mannerisms. Neither is grace a reconciliation with God, since there was never a separation.

Grace has nothing to do with anything that anyone else has ever done, nor with any outward activity on our part. Grace is an inner realization that we are *already* one with God, always have been and always will be, and that the only separation is a false belief in our own mind. Grace is simply the Truth of Being that which we are.

Some people appear to be born with an inherent sense of their unity with God and man. Many call this a "gift," and when we meet such people it does appear that they have been favored with a rare and precious gift. The Truth is, however, that we have all received this gift of grace. The difference is in the level of our awareness of it. It is difficult to understand why some persons appear more aware of this birthright than others. Those expressing this gift are rarely people of great learning, nor would they claim to be "masters." They simply see good, or God, in everyone they meet.

Surely, we have all known people like this. My Aunt Berth was such a person. Though she faithfully read her Bible, she was not a scholar. And if anyone had told her that she epitomized the "Christian life," she would have laughed at the thought, for she saw so much good in everyone else. She possessed an innate sense of love for all people, and all who knew her loved her in return. I would go to her when troubled and receive the assurance that everything would be all right. And it always was. Her prayers seemed to have greater impetus than "ordinary prayers." To me, she was a little closer to God than the rest of us.

While there are those like my aunt who do not concern themselves with grace because they are so busy expressing it, there are others who simply do not concern themselves. These are the people who go through life bound by the chains of cause and effect, unaware that they can lift themselves above this law by free will, unaware that there is an even higher expression of God's law than free will—grace.

If we were not born with the conscious awareness that we are under grace, we need not be discouraged. God told Moses His name (or nature) was "I am who I am."[14] This is the first person, present tense of the verb "to be." To live under grace, all we need do is "to be" who we are.

And if that does not come naturally, we can learn *how* to be.

Grace Is Meekness—Freedom From, and Freedom to Be

As Shadrach symbolized the meekness that results in spiritual power, we too are freed from all sense of the false and can express our true Self by developing this quality of meekness within ourselves.

Meekness is freedom from negation. It is a slate wiped clean. Preconceived beliefs and guilts bind us to the past and disrupt our present and future. Jealousy and suspicion lock us in a realm of fantasy. Freedom from these mental germs allows us the liberty to be ourselves.

Fear, also, is a malignancy of the mind, permitting the imagination to run rampant.

> *Imagination frames events unknown*
> *In wild fantastic shapes of hideous ruin,*
> *And what it fears creates.*[15]

As long as we fear, we are subject to that which we fear. Freedom from fear is our greatest protection, our most potent deterrent from harm. Even the fear of death, which Robert Browning called "the arch fear,"[16] must be removed. Only when we are free of this most universal fear, when we realize our eternality and see death as merely a shadow, are we free to fully live.

There is a story of a disciple of Mohammed who reported: "Master, my brothers have fallen asleep. I alone have remained awake to worship Allah."

Mohammed answered, "It would have been better had you fallen asleep if your worship consists of judging your brothers." Meekness is freedom not to judge.

Jesus admonished: "Judge not, that you be not judged. For with the judgment you pronounce you will be judged, and the measure you give will be the measure you get."[17]

Henry David Thoreau admitted, "For many years I was self-appointed inspector of snowstorms and rainstorms, and I did my duty faithfully."[18]

The freedom not to judge is liberating. To place upon ourselves the burden of determining the "why's" of actions and events beyond our understanding is an exhausting task. We have enough to do when we properly mind our own spiritual business.

As we express true meekness, we discover that freedom *from* invariably brings with it the absolute freedom to *be*.

Grace Is Unconditional Love

We, as parents, love our children. We love them no less when they act in an immature fashion, nor do we require that they perform particular acts to merit our love. We love them simply because they are our children.

According to Jesus, this is God's feeling for us. When we fail to achieve our highest potential, God does not love us less, nor does He require that we meet certain standards or take part in special rituals. God's love is unconditional. He knows what we are, even when we do not.

Forgiveness is an important aspect of love, closely aligned with grace. That we must forgive others (cease holding ourselves in bondage to that person or situation) is evident. There is no need for us to plead forgiveness for our own errors. Asking forgiveness is for our benefit, not God's. As far as God is concerned, there is never anything to forgive. Being God—absolute good—He sees only good. "Thou . . . art of purer eyes than to behold evil and canst not look on wrong,"[19] wrote the prophet Habakkuk, describing his God. If God saw less than good, then He would not be God, but a false deity such as King Nebuchadnezzar's creation of gold.

A friend once confessed that as a teenager she had stolen an object from a store. For twenty years she suffered—begging, pleading, cajoling God to forgive her, yet never feeling forgiven. Then one day she realized that she would not perform such an act now. She could not even conceive of such a thing. In that moment, she knew she was forgiven. "And strangely enough," she told me, "I recognized this as grace. There had never even been a need for me to ask forgiveness. All that was needed was that *I* change my mind."

There may be those who believe they are suffering a karmic debt, paying for some wrong committed in a past lifetime. Like my friend, all that is needed is to ask the question, "Would I perform such an act now?" If the answer is "no," then whatever the difficulty, I believe it is not karmic, for grace erases all debts—past and present.

"But what if I am suffering a karmic debt and don't know what I did to bring it about?" The answer is, be sure you are complying with the physical and mental laws of this present world. The concept of karma is sometimes used as justification for poor judgment. The next step is to apply love wherever the challenge might be, for there is no condition, whatever the cause, that enough love will not heal.

Grace Is Wisdom

If we are to live under the law of grace, we must apply wisdom in our lives. We may wonder how to go about achieving so lofty a goal. If it were necessary to strive for this, if it were beyond our reach, wisdom would not be a component of grace, for grace is a gift.

Wisdom, as opposed to knowledge, is inherent in all and applied as a result of controlling our thoughts. When we think only of good—God— the law of good operating in our lives annihilates all belief in so-called laws of disease, poverty, failure, loneliness.

It is *belief* in any concept of a law of disease that we must eliminate, not disease. It is *belief* in a law of poverty, *belief* in a law of failure, *belief* in a law of lovelessness from which we must be free. Why fight the effects when we can eliminate the root cause? Disease is an effect! It results from a false belief in a law of disease. Poverty is an effect! Failure is an effect! Lack of love is an effect!

Can you imagine God with the mumps? Can you imagine God complaining of inflation? Can you imagine God declaring bankruptcy? Can you imagine God in a divorce court? As children of God, we are of the same *ideal* of health, prosperity, success, and love. We must forget lack and think only of Truth.

We might say: "But I already have this problem. What can be done about this?" The answer is that God intends it for good. This in no way implies that God brought the situation about or that the condition itself is good. What it does mean is that regardless of the state in which we find ourselves, when we change our thoughts, good can and will result. By turning completely and absolutely to God, we are restored, and with Joseph, we affirm: *"You meant evil against me; but God meant it for good."*[20]

We may say, "But I have tried and nothing happens!"

Wisdom in its early stages is like an infant. We—each of us—are its parents. We give birth to the baby, but we do not grow the child. All our urgings do nothing. The conscious understanding of grace and its expression of wisdom grow on their own. We provide the food and drink of prayer and meditation. By nurturing our child with these, "he" grows in wisdom and stature, and we receive peace of mind, health, prosperity, success, harmony, and fellowship with God Himself.

Metanoia

A change of mind is the first step toward an acceptance of grace. The New Testament word *repentance* comes from the Latin *poena,* meaning "punishment."[21] This is a different word than the Greek *metanoia,* from which it was mistranslated.[22]

Metanoia has nothing to do with remorse, recrimination, or regret, but rather, refers to a transformation of the mind. When we change our minds, the outer circumstances of life change accordingly.

But we see good people suffer, and the humanity in us wonders why. Is there no protection? Are we the victims of chance? Fate? Karma? Is there no way to control our lives as physical beings? The answer is in Paul's words, "Do not be conformed to this world but be transformed by the renewal of your mind, that you may prove what is the will of God, what is good and acceptable and perfect."[23]

As long as we conform to the world—bow down to the golden idols of duality: good and bad, sickness and health, prosperity and poverty, success and failure, love and hate—we are subject to them. The moment we transform our minds and see only God—good—like Shadrach, Meshach, and Abednego, we are delivered from whatever fiery furnace we face. As we transform our minds, we remove our susceptibility.

Opportunity and Susceptibility

Picture in your imagination a grocery store. Visualize a group of perfect, beautifully formed melons on a display counter. People pass by and carelessly poke, pinch, and squeeze them. Each time pressure is applied, the melon is bruised and its protective covering weakened.

We might think of the consciousness as similar to one of these melons. It is perfect and beautifully formed. But thoughts of the world pass by and carelessly poke, pinch, and squeeze it—thoughts of fear, guilt, disease . . . and each negative thought bruises.

The bruised melons in the store we were visualizing are extremely vulnerable. Someone passes and lifts one. A soft, darkened area is touched, the rind gives way, and the fruit of the melon is exposed. Decomposition begins. Though not every melon will necessarily be affected in this way, each has become susceptible. If the right "squeeze" comes along, the covering, no longer strong, is subject to breakage.

Consciousness is much the same. It may be susceptible to disease, poverty, inharmonies, due to false concepts that have bruised it over the years—yet nothing may happen. Hopefully, we will escape the particular "squeeze" that destroys. But to trust the possibility is chancy. We never know when an especially strong "jab" will come along and expose us to a disorder.

The wisest course is to heal the bruises, to remove the susceptibility. And we can do this, for we are susceptible only so long as we "conform" to the beliefs of this world. This does not mean that we need to remove ourselves from the world. It does mean that we must change our minds and believe only in the law of good. Then we have done what the grocer cannot do for the melons. We have literally removed those bruised areas of susceptibility from our consciousness and restored it to its innate perfection.

We do this by recognizing only God, by "knowing" that we are already under grace, that this is the natural condition for us, and that anything less is the unnatural.

We have faith that the sun will rise tomorrow morning. We cannot conceive of it doing otherwise. When we have this same trust that we are under the Father's divine protection, then *nothing* can possibly harm us.

The Trumpet Sounds

> Lo! I tell you a mystery. We shall not all sleep, but we shall all be changed, in a moment, in the twinkling of an eye, at the last trumpet. For the trumpet will sound, and the dead will be raised imperishable, and we shall be changed. For this perishable nature must put on the imperishable, and this mortal nature must put on immortality. When the perishable puts on the imperishable, and the mortal puts on immortality, then shall come to pass the saying that is written:
>
> "Death is swallowed up in victory." [24]

This scripture is often read at funerals to signify the change that takes place at death. But we need not die to experience this change. We can "all be changed in a moment, in the twinkling of an eye." The trumpet of our own attitudes blows and changes from mortal thinking to immortal thinking, from death to eternal life. The perishable nature, the bruised part of our consciousness that has conformed to the world, is *transformed*, and *now,* right here on this Earth as human beings, we put on immortality.

This is grace.

Gratuities of Grace

1. You do not have to win God over. Grace is not a magic spell that God may or may not place on you. Grace is simply a decision to change your mind.

2. Know that when you develop the Shadrach, Meshach, and Abednego (meekness, love, and wisdom) within yourself, you have a

protecting angel who is with you in every fiery furnace you face, allowing you to walk through the flames, not only unharmed, but without even the scent of smoke about you.

3. Call forth Shadrach, Meshach, and Abednego from the inner recesses of your consciousness. Affirm their authority in your life; say, *My God is able to deliver me.* Deny the golden idols of appearance. Tell them, "You are nothing, a pretender, a misrepresentation!" Then speak to your own Nebuchadnezzar, your dominant will. Instruct him till he, too, sees only good. Claim God's guidance and protection in your life now.

4. Look for the good in others. Affirm: *I behold the Christ in you!*[25]

5. Pray and meditate. Do not be like the person who in an emergency could only remember, "Now I lay me. . . ." Prayer and meditation are powerful practices, but like all accomplishments of worth, they must be practiced properly and with regularity.

6. Exercise good judgment. The human body is subject to the laws of physics. Do not "try"

God. The chances are that you cannot handle snakes or drink poison substances. Though we are eternal beings, Earth is the best place for you and me right now. We must cooper-ate with its laws!

Chapter 12

Eternality

"Before Abraham was, I am."[1]

"I'm as old as my tongue and not quite as old as my teeth," my Aunt Beulah laughingly responded to my childish curiosity. Since that day many years ago I have heard responses to the query, "How old are you?" ranging from the frank, "I'm ____ years old and don't care who knows it!" to the equally frank, "It's none of your business!" My own answer to such a question is likely to be, "I don't know"—not because my birth certificate was misplaced or I have developed forgetfulness, but because I question the manner in which we measure age.

By what method should age be determined? Chronological time? Accomplishments? Love given or received?

Years are relative and limit us to that brief span of events that falls between human birth and death. One person may live a full, rich lifetime in a few years. Another may spend ninety years on this Earth and merely experience one year ninety times.

My favorite response to the question "How old are you?" came from a woman in a Unity class I attended. She was beautifully young looking, yet her personal knowledge of past events betrayed her appearance. Someone ventured the question, and without a moment's hesitation, she replied, "I'm as old as eternity and as young as this moment!"

George

My dear friend George epitomized this philosophy of agelessness. I was two years old when he came to work for our family. George was a man with such strength that he could easily raise the back of a car with his bare hands. Yet those same hands were as gentle as an angel's wing when lifting with monotonous regularity a frightened child (me) from her trap atop a barbed-wire fence.

George was thirty years old, he said; his sister had told him on his last visit to Louisiana. There was no reason to doubt the accuracy of this figure until the years passed and everyone grew older while George remained "thirty." Another fascinating fact about George was that while other people got sick, he remained healthy. When asked how he managed this, he explained that he was once employed by a doctor who gave him a shot to prevent all future illness. It had worked!

George never attended school. He could neither read nor write, except for his name, which I taught him to do during a brief period when I enjoyed playing the role of school teacher. Some might call him "ignorant." I think not.

George was unbound by the concept of years. He lived each moment to the fullest in the eternal now.

Some twenty-five years later he made his transition. He had worked all day. When he failed to appear for work the next morning, someone found him resting peacefully on his bed. Though birth records showed him to be past eighty, I am sure that in his heart George was still "thirty years old."

His passing was as natural as stepping through a doorway into another room. The only change was to those of us who remained behind. His joyous physical presence was no longer with us. For George, however, I feel sure that very little change occurred. The real Self, the essence of the man we loved, was and is exactly the same.

What Shall We Be?

"Beloved, we are God's children now; it does not yet appear what we shall be."[2]

At our present level of understanding, the event we call death seems a part of our experience. As humans have evolved, we have expanded our years as well as our capacity to enjoy them. We continue to do so. Surely one day the appearance of death, as we now know it, will no longer be a part of our experience. Now, however, the time comes (in much the same way in which we sometimes find it desirable to move from one house to another) that the soul finds the body it occupies no longer a suitable vehicle for its productive use. So it moves on.

A story is told about former President John Quincy Adams, who in his vintage years met an old friend as he slowly walked along the streets of Boston. The friend eagerly clasped his quavering hand and asked, "How is John Quincy Adams today?"

"John Quincy Adams is quite well, thank you," Mr. Adams replied. "But the house in which he lives at present is becoming dilapidated. It is tottering upon its foundations. Time and the seasons have nearly destroyed it. Its roof is pretty well worn out. Its walls are much shattered, and it trembles with every wind. The old tenement is becoming almost uninhabitable, and I think John Quincy Adams will have to move out of it soon. But he himself is quite well, quite well."

I recall sitting at the bedside of one I dearly loved who in advanced years moved easily from this consciousness to another. It seemed as natural and as beautiful as the birth of a new baby or a leaf falling from a tree in the autumn. Her life was full and an inspiration for all. There was little sadness. Those she left behind felt as did Benjamin Franklin at the death of his brother, "Why should we grieve that a new child is born among the immortals?"[3]

Yet death is not always kind. Why do some suffer? we wonder. Why are some snuffed out in the prime of life or before they have the opportunity to fully experience life?

Well-meaning metaphysicians sometimes feel the necessity to resolve these questions. Though we should do all we can to give prayerful and loving support to one in need, especially beholding the person's indwelling Christ, we should remember that each human being has as his or her birthright the gift of free will. We cannot, we *must* not, attempt to interfere with or determine the "why's" of another's existence—the going out or coming in.[4] This remains between the individual and God. We can and must, however, work out our own destiny. But what is our destiny? All evidence points to the fact that it is something far greater than anything that we, with the physical mechanism called a "brain," can perceive. We receive hints when for brief moments the mystery is unveiled for the soul to glimpse. But for the Adam-man, clothed in his garments of skin,[5] the mystery of the tree of life at the east of the garden of Eden remains guarded by the cherubim and the flaming sword,[6] and to our human vision, "it does not yet appear what we shall be."

We Are Eternal Now

Many sincere Christians are still held captive by the old concept that eternity is something to look forward to in the future, after this life is over. Donne, in his *Book of Devotions*, wrote, "Eternity is not an everlasting flux of time, but time is as a short parenthesis in a long period."[7] Sir Thomas Brown echoed this thought when he wrote, "The created world is but a small parenthesis in eternity."[8]

A parenthesis in eternity . . . Once we loosen our limiting beliefs in beginnings and endings we are freed to live fully in the present moment. Psychologist Carl Jung described the belief in immortality as good medicine and the very best mental hygiene.[9] I can think of nothing more inspiring than for those I have known, well past what the world regards as their "prime," to continue lifelong work or embark on challenging new careers.

My friend Alice had always wanted to attend

college, but she was past sixty-five when she began her first class. Friends laughingly chided, "Don't you realize you'll be almost seventy years old when you graduate?"

"True," Alice replied, "but in four years I'll be almost seventy anyway. If I start now, I'll be seventy with a degree. If not, I'll just be seventy."

Almost everyone is familiar with the story of the report of Mark Twain's death and his quip that the report was greatly exaggerated. A less famous man found himself in the same predicament. The "deceased" rushed to the newspaper office demanding that something be done. "I'm sorry," the editor informed him. "It's too late. The best I can do is put your name in the 'Birth Column' tomorrow morning and give you a fresh new start!"

As we grow in our conviction of eternality, we are truly given a fresh new start each and every day. When we know the Truth that we are immortal beings, natives of eternity, we lose our fear of beginnings. We realize that nothing is ever lost, nor is it ever too late to begin anew.

This is the teaching of Jesus. He did not postpone heaven to some time and place in the future. His words were simply, "Behold, the kingdom of God is in the midst of [within] you."[10]

Charles Fillmore's Demonstration

Charles Fillmore believed that it was possible to achieve eternal life in the body. He never gave up his effort and faith that he would achieve this goal. For *Unity Magazine*, he wrote:

> Some of my friends think that it is unwise for me to make this public statement of my conviction that I shall overcome death, that if I fail it will be detrimental to the Unity cause. I am not going to admit any such possibility.[11]

As a result of a childhood accident, Charles Fillmore's leg was crippled and his right side weakened. His hearing and vision were impaired. The man who set out to prove the scientific principles of practical Christianity was far from a perfect physical specimen. After studying and practicing Truth for only a short time, he noted that the constant pain he suffered had ceased. Gradually, his hearing and vision improved. The right side of his body grew stronger, and he was eventually able to do away with the brace that had been his constant companion for years. Well into his tenth decade Charles Fillmore was lecturing, writing, touring the country. He continued to believe in and seek to prove his perfected body. At age ninety-two, he wrote:

> I do not claim that I have yet attained that perfection but I am on my way. My leg is still out of joint but it is improving as I continue to work under the direction and guidance of Spirit. [11]

At ninety-three he made his transition. Can anyone seriously doubt that he achieved his goal? When he began his spiritual quest in the spring of 1886, the medical prognosis for this sick, crippled man was far from promising. Yet he lived on this Earth an additional sixty-two healthy and productive years, teaching and practicing the Truth he believed in. I have a feeling that while Mr. Fillmore's family and friends were still attempting to assimilate the fact of his passing, he was in their midst with his perfected body, joyfully exclaiming: "I made it! I knew I would!" It may have been with some surprise that he noted the sadness of his loved ones. Perhaps he was perplexed at their inability to perceive his presence among them and share his joy. Had he not taught and told them what he would do?

Then surely he realized that if there was a flaw, it was not in his demonstration, but in the limited human vision.

We can be as sure as Charles Fillmore that we, too, will continue eternally. Life is. It is as simple, yet as profound as that. And life inevitably clothes itself in appropriate garb.

Jesus told us:

> "Do not be anxious about . . . your body, what you shall put on. . . . Consider the lilies, how they grow; they neither toil nor spin; yet I tell you, even Solomon in all his glory was not arrayed like one of these. But if God so clothes the grass which is alive in the field today and tomorrow is thrown into the oven, how much more will he clothe you!" [12]

My Assurance

While in his early fifties my father-in-law, Cedric Pounders, experienced a stroke. He had been an attorney, a man with an active mind and body. For the last nineteen years of his life, though his mind remained alert, his speech and vision were severely affected and his right side paralyzed, making it impossible for him to move about except in a wheelchair.

Never have I known a more patient person. He bore numerous challenges during these years— with cheerfulness and without complaint. He loved being with people and was a typically doting grandfather to our children, though his condition prevented his partaking of that role in the fullest physical sense.

His transition was quiet. When the nurse came to remove his breakfast tray, she thought he had fallen asleep. Though we missed him, we were grateful that he was at last freed from the prison his body had become.

One night about a year later, I dreamed I was in a strange room. Suddenly, I saw Cedric standing before me. Standing! I had *never* seen him stand! He was vigorous with health and vitality and was smiling happily. Quickly, my husband Frank and I ran to Cedric, throwing our arms about him as the three of us laughed and shed tears of joy.

Cedric then took us to a conference room where it was decided that we be allowed to witness the regeneration process taking place. We entered an area much like a hospital recovery room. The lighting was dim. Each of the tablelike beds was occupied by a man or woman in various stages of recovery from the shock of "death." Most were still sleeping. Though few had serious difficulties, some appeared stunned and unsure of their whereabouts. On waking, they were cared for by attendants who explained what had taken place and assured them that they were safe. As we watched, the attendants repeated words of Truth, stating over and over that this was their Real Body, that the experience they had undergone was just that—a passing event with no enduring significance or importance. After a brief period most seemed satisfied and were helped from their beds and led from the room.

I watched a man wake in terror. I noted a

gaping, scarlet incision in his chest area. An attendant was immediately with him, assuring him that he was alive, healthy, with all unpleasant experiences behind him. He looked as if he were waking from a dream. At first he seemed unconvinced, but as he listened, the wound began to reverse itself. It did not heal in the ordinary way by slowly forming protective scar tissue. The healing process was more like watching a movie film of an injury taking place, played backward. As we watched, the wound simply disappeared, leaving clear, clean flesh where the incision had been. It was my impression that I was observing the manner in which healing of the physical body also takes place without death having occurred—first the mental, then the physical.

I observed one who was not so receptive to the Truth told him. It seemed he had been there longer than usual because of firmly accepting and believing in the reality of a long and difficult physical illness. The wound on his forehead had partially vanished, but traces remained. As he occasionally moaned or cried out, the wound deepened and turned an angry shade of crimson. Attendants again lovingly, but insistently affirmed with him that there was nothing of his past to fear or hold him, that he was indeed free and whole. As they spoke, the healing process resumed.

Though I know some persons might explain this as "a meaningless dream," a form of wish fulfillment, I can only say that to me it was as real as any experience I have ever known. I am not a seeker of phenomena. I do not possess extraordinary powers, nor do I claim that this was a vision. It was a dream. I was asleep, not in a trance. I do believe, however, that when the conscious mind is stilled, as it is in sleep, we are often receptive to ideas that come to us from beyond the scope of our physical senses.

I share this in the hope that it may offer some reassurance to others who have lost loved ones or who might be facing physical challenges themselves. I have no doubt that I was in the presence of my father-in-law, that he was the same person I had known for fifteen years, and that he was well and happy in a recognizable, perfected body, vibrant with life. I believe also that through love he made the effort to let us know that this was so.

Proof of Immortality

"Nature does not know extinction; all it knows is transformation. Everything science has taught me, and continues to teach me, strengthens my belief in a continuity of our spiritual existence after death."[13] These are not the words of a theologian, but of the scientist, Werner Van Braun. The poet Goethe expressed the same belief. "I am fully convinced that the soul is indestructible, and that its activities will continue through eternity. It is like the sun, which to our eyes, seems to set in night; but has really gone to diffuse its light elsewhere."[14]

Thinkers of all ages have been convinced of the immortality of the soul. Now, however, there is ample scientific evidence, confirmed by objective medical experts, from statements of people reported clinically dead, then revived, to convince all but the most skeptical of the validity of this belief. The statements are unmistakably similar.[15]

The strongest proof of our immortality, however, comes not from scientists, philosophers, or poets, but, as does all Truth, from within ourselves. Since earliest ages man has recognized that something within him defies the senses and demands continuity. Primitive man felt this and buried his beloved dead with their favorite possessions. The only possible purpose would have been that he hoped for them to be used again when the owner awakened.

Man is a creature of desires, and his Creator has provided for the fulfillment of each of them. How cruel, how illogical it would be if God should plant within the heart of His most loved creation the greatest of all desires—immortality—only to deny it!

The story is told of the Egyptian architect Onidus who was commissioned by Pharaoh to build a lighthouse at the mouth of the Nile.

According to his assignment, he engraved the name of Pharaoh on the cement covering the outside. Years passed and the wind and rain beat at the cement until Pharaoh's name was worn away. Only then was the name of the architect Onidus uncovered, deeply engraved within the masonry beneath.

As we study The Gospels, we discover the greatest of all demonstrations of life. It begins with the empty tomb. How puzzling! Jesus had been crucified. He was dead on the cross and placed in a tomb belonging to Joseph of Arimathea.[16] Yet his body was gone. Vanished!

When we look beyond the surface of this story, we see that the tomb had to be empty, just as the mortal body is empty when the soul has departed. With our inner vision, we stand in the garden as did Mary Magdalene and we, too, come face-to-face with Jesus, clothed in his eternal identity—the risen Christ. So pure was his belief in life that even to the limited human vision he was clearly recognizable.

The name *Christ* is engraved deep within the soul of each of us. Christ is the Architect of our being and our eternal Self. And the words that Christ Jesus spoke to his disciples are spoken to each of us as well—"Lo, I am with you always."[17]

This is indeed God's greatest law of love.

Life Savers

1. Know yourself as eternal. Never allow false appearances of lack, sickness, or age to prevent you from expressing the person you

truly are—an eternal, immortal being going through a wonderful human experience. The world will try to convince you that this is not so, but you must refuse to believe it. You dwell in eternity now. Know with Emerson, "that which we commonly call man . . . does not, as we know him, represent himself, but misrepresents himself."[18] As you think of the Truth about who you are, put aside old outmoded concepts that misrepresent you as a mortal creature, preparing for death from the instant of birth, and take on the radiant, expressing, eternal being which is your true identity.

2. Speak words of life. You will receive arguments from acquaintances, loved ones, even the television set. Race beliefs do not die without a struggle. You must, however, recognize them as the lies they are and mentally or verbally deny all words contrary to life. "Sing them over again to me, wonderful words of life."[19] Speak them, sing them, shout them! Each person who follows the admonition of this wonderful old hymn lifts not only himself, but his brother and sister

as well. Affirm the Truth that you are now living forever.

3. Then act as if it were true. It is, you know. It is never too late for you to do or be whatever you want. Every enriching experience becomes a part of your eternal identity and is with you forever.

"We sleep, but the loom of life never stops and the pattern, which was weaving when the sun went down, is weaving when it comes up tomorrow."[20]

ACTIVITIES

The purpose of this Activities section is to assist the student, whether working alone or in a group setting, to gain the greatest possible growth from *Laws of Love*.

Each chapter of *Laws of Love* contains three Activities features: Questions for Discussion or Study, Affirmations and Denials, and Questions for Self-Realization.

Questions covering the chapter are provided and can be used for discussion in a group or for individual home study.

A series of affirmations and denials pertinent to the subject of the chapter is offered. It is suggested that the affirmations be spoken firmly, enthusiastically, and with exaggerated gestures. The denials should be spoken lightly, as "throwaway lines." It is also suggested that the student write personal affirmations and denials in addition to using those in the activities.

Answering the questions for Self-realization is an introspective activity, yet one that can be productively shared by those who wish to discuss these inner attitudes regarding the subject of the chapter. These questions, whether considered individually or with a group, should result in a greater awareness of the student's thoughts and feelings regarding self, others, and the world in which we live.

Chapter 1

Patterns

Questions for Discussion or Study

1. How does Truth differ from fact?
2. What is meant by the statement attributed to Plato, "In heaven is laid up a pattern which he who chooses may behold, and beholding, set his house in order"?
3. Who is the "only begotten Son"?
4. How is "our world" created?
5. What did Jesus mean by the statement, "If two of you agree on earth about anything they ask, it will be done for them by my Father in heaven"? (Mt. 18:19)
6. Explain the importance of "decision" and "desire" in making a demonstration.

Affirmations and Denials

1. I deny and overcome past beliefs in limitation.

2. *I am a good and worthy human being. This is the truth about me.*
3. *I feel good about myself.*
4. *My body is good; my body is my friend. I say to my body: "You are a good body! I love and appreciate you!"*
5. *My environment is good. My environment is my friend. I say to my environment: "You are good. I love and appreciate you!"*
6. Nothing can hold me back. *My life is getting better every day!*

Questions for Self-Realization

1. What is my *real* concept of myself?
   my body . . .
   my intellect . . .
   my environment . . .
   my creative ability . . .
   my heredity . . .
2. How do my concepts of myself differ from the pattern which God created?
3. What steps can I take to bring these into harmony?

———————◄O►———————

Chapter 2

Abundance

Questions for Discussion or Study

1. What is the real meaning of "prosperity"?
2. Discuss some effective ways to still the body and mind.
3. How important is it to have specific goals?
4. What is meant by "the marriage between the masculine and feminine natures," and how is this brought about?
5. How can we relate to Jesus' practice of giving thanks in advance?
6. How do we determine the action which is necessary to the completion of a demonstration?
7. In what ways do we fail to "release" our desire to that Power which knows how to bring its fulfillment into being?
8. How can we increase our willingness to receive?

Affirmations and Denials

1. *I affirm that I now have all that I desire.*
2. I deny any appearance to the contrary.
3. *I give thanks that I have already received my good.*
4. *I give, and it is given to me.*
5. There is no loss in Spirit, and I am pure Spirit.

Questions for Self-Realization

1. What does the word *prosperity* really mean to me?
2. Are there any good things of which I do not feel worthy?
3. If so, why?
4. How can I change this?

————————◄O►————————

Chapter 3

Compensation

Questions for Discussion or Study

1. What is meant by "the law of compensation"?
2. In what ways can we block the working of the law of compensation?
3. What is meant by the allegory of the birth of Seth to Adam and Eve? (Gen. 4:25)
4. What is meant by "ours by right of consciousness"?
5. How much does God compensate?

Affirmations and Denials

1. There is no loss in Spirit, and I am pure Spirit.
2. *This is the day which the Lord has made. I do rejoice and I'm glad in it.*
3. That which is mine in Spirit will come to me. There is no power that can keep it from me.
4. *God is my generous parent, and He gives to me tenfold for any seeming lack.* He overcompensates for even the appearance of loss.

5. *I give of myself and my goods, and I am over-compensated.*

Questions for Self-Realization

1. Are there any areas of my life in which I feel I have been cheated?
2. What negative attitudes do I harbor to block my compensation?
3. Have I received more than I "earned" in any area of my life?
4. Am I able to graciously accept this as God's loving gift to me?

Chapter 4

Release

Questions for Discussion or Study

1. What are some of the spiritual purposes in Moses' command to keep the Sabbath day holy?

2. What are the probable results of randomly discussing the things closest to our hearts?

3. How does "forgiveness" relate to the law of release?

4. Discuss some techniques for effective forgiveness.

5. How is "release" a vital step in every demonstration? Can you share a personal experience as an example of this?

6. What is the effect of possessiveness?

Affirmations and Denials

1. *I rest in the Lord. I relax, release, and rest in the knowledge that the Lord, the Law of my being, knows how to bring all things about.*

2. I renounce old concepts that have no purpose in my life.

3. I forgive myself of all past errors.

4. I am no longer the same person who made those errors, and I can no longer blame a person who does not exist.

5. *Now that I know better, I do better!*

6. *I freely forgive and turn loose of all grudges.*

Questions for Self-Realization

1. Is there any person, place, animal, thing, or event for which I hold hard feelings or a lack of forgiveness?
2. Is there anything for which I have not forgiven myself?
3. Am I clinging to any person or any thing which I should release to God's care?
4. Am I clinging to any negative attitude which I should release to God's care?
5. Am I being possessive in any area of my life?

————◄○►————

Chapter 5

Nonresistance

Questions for Discussion or Study

1. What is nonresistance?
2. What attitudes compose nonresistance?
3. How can resistance lead to inappropriate action? Can you give any examples?

4. Does nonresistance act from strength or weakness? In what ways?
5. What place does "honesty with self" play in practicing nonresistance?

Affirmations and Denials

1. I do not resist evil. I overcome evil with good.
2. *I know the Truth, and the Truth sets me free.*
3. I harbor no ill feelings toward any person, place, or thing. *God's love and life flow through all of my experiences.*
4. My attitudes are free of ill-will, and I act from a point of strength and wisdom within.
5. I know that God loves me, and there is no power except the power of God's love in my life and in my world.

Questions for Self-Realization

1. Am I experiencing any negative feelings? List these feelings completely as possible.
2. Are there any areas in which I am experiencing resistance? (Remember: Resistance is an attitude, not an action.)
3. How can I free myself of resistance?

◄○►

Chapter 6

Perfection

Questions for Discussion or Study

1. How can we reconcile Jesus' statement that "you, therefore, must be perfect, as your heavenly Father is perfect" (Mt. 5:48) with the recognition of our shortcomings and errors?
2. When we make affirmations of Truth are we lying to ourselves? How do you feel about this?
3. How would you define the difference between "me" and "I"? Between "personality" and "individuality"?
4. What should we do regarding "personality"?
5. What is the spiritual meaning of "the atonement"?
6. How does "perfection" express in our daily lives?

Affirmations and Denials

1. *I am healthy. Every part of my body—physical and mental—is vibrant and strong.*
2. God is neither mentally nor physically ill, and I am His child, made in His image and likeness.
3. *I am wealthy. I have access to all the substance in the universe. My every need is met.*
4. *I am creative. Ideas are mine through divine inspiration. I am guided and directed at all times.*
5. *I am loved and I am loving. Everyone likes me, and I see only good in others. My relationships are harmonious and joyful.*
6. God is not poor or lacking in creative ideas or love. *I am His child, made in His image and likeness, and all that my Father has is mine.*
7. *I am a perfect spiritual being, joyously expressing the wonderful human experience.*

Questions for Self-Realization

1. How do I really feel that God sees me?
2. How do I really see myself—my body, my affairs, my environment, my relationships?

3. How can I make my concept of "me" harmonize with God's idea of "me"?

————◀○▶————

Chapter 7

Order

Questions for Discussion or Study

1. What does "order" mean to you?
2. Can we depend on the "natural order" of life? Give some examples of this.
3. If we do not like the condition of our outer world, how can we change it?
4. Describe some basic needs of all human beings.
5. What part can words play in creating or correcting the conditions of our lives?
6. How does the soul or mind affect our health, prosperity, relationships, and creativity?
7. How do we reestablish order in our lives?

Affirmations and Denials

1. Dis-ease, dis-appointment, dis-order have no place in my life.

2. *I am capable and "pre-dispositioned" for "ease" and "order" in my body, thoughts, and emotions. I am oriented toward that which is good and perfect.*

3. *I am effective and efficient in all that I do. I courageously go forward to meet my appointed good.*

4. "I am a child of God; therefore, I do not inherit sickness." (Myrtle Fillmore)

5. I am a child of God; therefore, I do not inherit poverty, failure, or a bad disposition.

6. *I experience perfect circulation, perfect assimilation, and perfect elimination in every aspect of my life. I give that which I have to give, and good flows back to me.* I keep that which is needful; I rid myself of that which is no longer beneficial to my well-being.

7. *I affirm divine order!*

Questions for Self-Realization

1. In what ways do I *think* I am not expressing order?
2. In what ways do I *feel* I am not expressing order?
3. Do my thoughts and feelings regarding order and disorder in my life agree?
4. If not, what does this mean?

———————◄○►———————

Chapter 8

Creative Expression

Questions for Discussion or Study

1. Is creative expression essential to everyone? Explain.
2. Explain the three steps of the law of creativity—mind, idea, and expression.
3. What are some of the ways in which you are creative?

4. What place does "tenacity" and "initiative" have in creativity?
5. What is the part of "imagination" in creativity?
6. What is the mind? What is the brain? How do they differ?

Affirmations and Denials

1. I do not react to appearances. I freely let go all thoughts less than Truth. I am no longer bound by the false belief that I am in any way limited.
2. *I am a child of joy, a child of good. Through my creativity, I express my love for everyone in the world.*
3. *In touch with my creative center, I am helping.*
4. *I will smile and be pleasant in my every word and action as I joyfully and caringly put into practice God's creative ideas.*

Questions for Self-Realization

1. If I could do or be anything in the world, what would it be?

2. Am I doing or being this or its equivalent now? If not, why?
3. If no, is this reason really valid?

———————◀○▶———————

Chapter 9

Divine Discontent

Questions for Discussion or Study

1. What is the place of "divine discontent" in the evolvement of humankind?
2. What is the place of "divine discontent" in our individual lives? Can you share a personal experience?
3. What might Jesus have meant by his statement from the Beatitudes: "Blessed are those who mourn, for they shall be comforted"? (Mt. 5:4)
4. How would you distinguish between "dissatisfaction" and "divine discontent"?
5. What are some results of impulsiveness? Of procrastination?

6. What is the metaphysical meaning of "hell," and how is it beneficial to us?

Affirmations and Denials

1. I am not disturbed by feelings of discontent. Discontent is beneficial!
2. *Divine discontent is a gift of God, an expression of His confidence in me.*
3. *I am a radiant, glowing spark of light with limitless possibilities.*
4. I have no doubts as to my capabilities. God trusts me, and who am I to question God's trust?
5. There is nothing that the Father and I together cannot accomplish!

Questions for Self-Realization

1. Are there some areas of my life where I feel I am not living up to my full potential?
2. If yes, list some of those areas.
3. If yes, why?
4. Is this answer really valid?

Chapter 10

Free Will

Questions for Discussion or Study

1. Over what do we really have dominion? How?
2. How does the faculty of will act in our lives?
3. How can we deal with the prevalent false beliefs of the world in which we live?
4. How do our words take form? Is it necessary to take action on this physical plane? Explain your answer.
5. In what ways might we program the length of our lives?

Affirmations and Denials

1. I do not blame fate, karma, environment, or heredity for any situation. They are nothing. I alone choose my lot in life.
2. I cannot change the reactions of other persons, but I have dominion over my own thoughts, feelings, words, and thus, my world.
3. I cannot change the past, but I can change

the way I think, feel, and speak regarding the events of the past. I see the past as positive experience that has brought me to this present moment of good.

4. I refuse to accept the prejudices and fears of others. *I am a child of God, and I think as my Parent thinks.*

5. *I am an uncommon person, a child of God, in control of my life and all of my affairs.*

6. *I speak with authority, for my word carries weight and is far-reaching. The words that I speak are constructive and true.*

Questions for Self-Realization

1. Are there areas of my life in which I am not using my gift of "free will"?
2. If so, why?
3. Is this answer really valid?

Chapter 11

Grace

Questions for Discussion or Study

1. What is the spiritual significance of the story of Shadrach, Meshach, and Abednego (Daniel 3) in our own lives?
2. How would you describe the working of grace from a spiritual point of view?
3. How would you define spiritual "meekness"?
4. What are some of the aspects of "unconditional love"?
5. In what way is wisdom a component of grace?
6. How do we follow Paul's admonition, "Do not be conformed to this world but be transformed by the renewal of your mind"? (Rom. 12:2)
7. How do we become susceptible to disease, poverty, and inharmonies? How can we overcome such susceptibilities?

Affirmations and Denials

1. *I look for and see the good in all things.*
2. *I behold the Christ in you! I behold the Christ in myself!*
3. I say to all negative appearances, "You are nothing, a pretender, a misrepresentation."
4. *God's guidance and protection are mine now!*
5. *My mind is changed, and I am transformed!*
6. *I live under the law of grace, and all is well!*

Questions for Self-Realization

1. Do I love others without qualifications? If not, whom do I not love?
2. Do I love myself without qualification?
3. If either of the above answers is "no," why is this the case? Does this benefit me in any way?
4. How can I change this restrictive attitude?

―――――――◄○►―――――――

Chapter 12

Eternality

Questions for Discussion or Study

1. How old are you spiritually? How is that age determined?
2. If you did not know your chronological age, how old would you be?
3. How can we deal with the facts regarding the life, lack of health, or death of others?
4. What was meant by Sir Thomas Brown when he wrote, "The created world is but a small parenthesis in eternity"?
5. How do we strengthen our personal belief in eternal life?

Affirmations and Denials

1. Time and age have no power over me. The illusion of death has no power over me.
2. *I am as old as eternity and as young as this moment!*

3. *I am destined for something far greater than I have yet imagined!*
4. I do not postpone heaven to a time and place in the future. *My heaven exists right here and right now!*
5. *"I fairly sizzle with zeal and enthusiasm and spring forth with a mighty faith to do the things that ought to be done by me."* (Written by Charles Fillmore in his 93rd year.)
6. *I affirm the Truth that I am now living forever.*

Questions for Self-Realization

1. How do I feel about "old people"?
2. Do I really believe that life is eternal?
3. If so, what is my concept of it?
4. How does this concept of eternal life make me feel?

REFERENCES

All Bible references are from the Revised Standard Version, unless otherwise noted.

Introduction

1. Romans 13:10 (KJV).
2. Kate Louise Roberts, *Hoyt's New Cyclopedia of Practical Quotations,* (New York and London: Funk and Wagnalls Company, 1922), p. 319.
3. Ernest Holmes, *Science of Mind* magazine, "Discover a Richer Life," Issue Unknown, (published by Institute of Religious Science, Los Angeles, California).
4. Ralph Waldo Emerson, "Essays and English Traits," "Compensation," (New York: P. F. Collier & Son Co., *The Harvard Classics* [edited by Charles W. Eliot], Volume V, 1909), p. 89.
5. Charles Fillmore, *Christian Healing* (Lee's Summit, Mo.: Unity School of Christianity, 1968), p. 130.
6. Matthew 19:26.
7. Galatians 6:7.

Patterns—Chapter 1

1. Proverbs 23:7 (KJV).
2. James Dillet Freeman, *The Story of Unity* (Unity Village, Mo.: Unity Books), p. 47.
3. Oliver Wendell Holmes, "The Chambered Nautilus," St. 5 (from *Hoyt's New Cyclopedia of Practical Quotations*, [New York and London: Funk and Wagnalls Company, 1922]).
4. Psalm 11:4 (paraphrased).
5. Frederich Bailes, *Hidden Power for Human Problems* (Englewood Cliffs, N. J.: Prentice Hall, Inc., 1957), pp. 1–3.
6. Original source unknown, quoted from Emma Curtis Hopkins, *High Mysticism*, (Cornwall Bridge, Connecticut: High Watch Fellowship), p. 5.
7. 1 Corinthians 15:44.
8. Spenser, "An Hymn in Honour of Beauty," L. 132 (from *Hoyt's New Cyclopedia of Practical Quotations*).
9. Charles Fillmore, *The Revealing Word* (Unity Village, Mo.: Unity Books), p. 187.
10. *Ibid.*, p. 62.
11. Matthew 18:19.

12. Matthew 12:25.
13. *Dallas Morning News* (Dallas, Texas: The A. H. Belo Corporation, Publisher, Monday, July 18, 1977), p. 2A.
14. *Webster's New Twentieth Century Dictionary of the English Language Unabridged* (Cleveland and New York: The World Publishing Company, Second Edition, 1963), p. 470.
15. H. Emilie Cady, *Lessons in Truth* (Unity Village, Mo.: Unity Books), p. 78.
16. John 4:35.
17. Psalm 46:10.
18. Exodus 20:5 (paraphrased).

Abundance—Chapter 2

1. Luke 12:32.
2. Matthew 14: 13–20 (paraphrased).
3. Matthew 14:13–21; Mark 6:32–44; Luke 9:10–17; John 6:1–13.
4. *Webster's New Twentieth Century Dictionary of the English Language Unabridged* (Cleveland and New York: The World Publishing Company, Second Edition, 1963), p. 1446.
5. Matthew 11:28.

6. John 14:27.
7. Mark 6:31.
8. Charles Fillmore, *The Revealing Word* (Unity Village, Mo.: Unity Books), p. 166.
9. James Dillet Freeman, *The Story of Unity* (Unity Village, Mo.: Unity Books), p. 193.
10. Ring Lardner, "How to Write Short Stories," (from Charles Hurd, *A Treasury of Great American Quotations* [Chicago, Illinois: J. G. Ferguson Publishing Co., 1968]), p. 284.
11. Matthew 14:19.
12. Charles Fillmore, *op. cit.*, p. 29.
13. *Ibid.*, p. 75.
14. Matthew 5:37.
15. John 11:28–44.
16. Malachi 3:10.
17. Ephesians 6:13.
18. Mark 4:26–28.
19. Zechariah 4:6.

Compensation—Chapter 3

1. Joel 2:25.
2. Ralph Waldo Emerson, "Essays and English Traits," "Compensation," (New York: P. F.

Collier & Son Co., *The Harvard Classics* [edited by Charles W. Eliot] Volume V, 1909), p. 89.

3. Ecclesiastes 11:1.
4. Charles Fillmore, *The Revealing Word* (Unity Village, Mo.: Unity Books), p. 39.
5. Matthew 6:1.
6. Hebrews 13:2. (NRSV)
7. Genesis 4:8.
8. Charles Fillmore, *Metaphysical Bible Dictionary* (Unity Village, Mo.: Unity Books, 1931), p. 12.
9. *Ibid.*, p. 135.
10. Matthew 26:41.
11. Genesis 4:25.
12. Charles Fillmore, *op. cit.*, p. 584.
13. Genesis 4:12.
14. Matthew 5:18.
15. Galatians 6:7.
16. Luke 6:38.
17. *The Dallas Morning News*, Editorial (Dallas, Texas: The A. H. Belo Corp., Publisher, Wednesday, March 1, 1978), p. 2D.
18. Ralph Waldo Emerson, *op. cit.*, p. 89.
19. 2 Corinthians 12:7.

20. Joel 2:25–26.
21. Genesis 6:9.
22. Psalm 118:24.
23. Ralph Waldo Emerson, *loc. cit.*
24. John R. Sweney and Theodosia Smith, "I See Abundance Everywhere," *Unity Song Selections* (Unity Village, Mo.: Unity School of Christianity, 1941), p. 166.
25. Matthew 5:3–12.

Release—Chapter 4

1. Genesis 2:2.
2. *Webster's New Twentieth Century Dictionary of the English Language Unabridged* (Cleveland and New York: The World Publishing Company, Second Edition, 1963), p. 1525.
3. Elizabeth Sand Turner, *Let There Be Light* (Unity Village, Mo.: Unity Books, 1954), p. 220.
4. Charles Fillmore, *The Revealing Word* (Unity Village, Mo.: Unity Books), p. 178.
5. Matthew 22:21.
6. Exodus 20:8.
7. Carlyle, "Sartor Resartus," Bk. III, Ch. III (from

Hoyt's New Cyclopedia of Practical Quotations, Kate Louise Roberts, [New York and London: Funk and Wagnalls Company, 1922]).

8. John 10:10.
9. Charles Fillmore, *The Twelve Powers* (Unity Village, Mo.: Unity Books), p. 144.
10. *Webster's New Twentieth Century Dictionary of the English Language Unabridged, op. cit.*, p. 1640.
11. *Ibid.*, p. 1593.
12. Matthew 6:14.
13. Psalm 37:7 (KJV).
14. Matthew 18:19–20.
15. Henry Wadsworth Longfellow, "Tales of a Wayside Inn," "The Student's Tale," Pt. I, (from *Hoyt's New Cyclopedia of Practical Quotations*).

Nonresistance—Chapter 5

1. Matthew 5:39; Romans 12:21.
2. Edwin Markham, "Outwitted," (from Charles Hurd, *A Treasury of Great American Quotations* [Chicago, Illinois: J. G. Ferguson Publishing Co., 1968]), p. 220.

3. Matthew 21:12–13; Mark 11:15–17; Luke 19:45–46; John 2:13–17.

4. Matthew 16:19.

5. Solon, (from Kate Louise Roberts, *Hoyt's New Cyclopedia of Practical Quotations* [New York and London: Funk and Wagnalls Company, 1922]), p. 638.

6. Dr. William R. Parker and Elaine St. Johns, *Prayer Can Change Your Life* (Englewood Cliffs, N.J.: Prentice-Hall, Inc., 1957).

7. Source unknown.

8. Ralph Waldo Emerson, "Essays and English Traits," "Circles," (New York: P. F. Collier & Son Co., *The Harvard Classics* [edited by Charles W. Eliot], Volume V. 1909), p. 162.

9. Job 3:25.

10. Woodrow Wilson, in an address in Convention Hall, Philadelphia, May 10, 1915 (from *Hoyt's New Cyclopedia of Practical Quotations*).

11. Matthew 5:29–30.

12. Matthew 4:7.

13. John Ruskin, "The Eagles' Nest," Lecture IX (from *Hoyt's New Cyclopedia of Practical Quotations*).

14. Omar Khayyam, Rubaiyat, Fitzgerald's trans.,

(from *Hoyt's New Cyclopedia of Practical Quotations*), p. 738.
15. John 8:32.
16. Epictetus, *Discourses*, Bk. II, Ch. XVI (from *Hoyt's New Cyclopedia of Practical Quotations*).

Perfection—Chapter 6

1. Matthew 5:48.
2. Walt Whitman, "Song of the Universal," (from Charles Hurd, *A Treasury of Great American Quotations* [Chicago, Illinois: J. G. Ferguson Publishing Co., 1968]), p. 148.
3. *The World Almanac and Book of Facts 1999* (World Almanac Books, Mahwah, New Jersey, 1998), p. 862.
4. Charles Fillmore, *The Revealing Word* (Unity Village, Mo.: Unity Books), p. 202.
5. John 9:6.
6. Robert Browning, "Paracelsus," Part I (from *Masterpieces of Religious Verse*, [New York: Harper & Brothers, 1948]), p. 431.
7. H. Emilie Cady, *Lessons in Truth*, (Unity Village, Mo.: Unity Books, 1999), pp. 88–89.
8. 1 Corinthians 13:12.

9. Maurice Nicoll, *Psychological Commentaries on the Teaching of Gurdjieff and Ouspensky,* (London: Vincent Stuart, 1957) Volume I.

10. Proverbs 11:29.

11. *Webster's New Twentieth Century Dictionary of the English Language Unabridged* (Cleveland and New York: The World Publishing Company, Second Edition, 1963), p. 1338.

12. Matthew 6:22–23.

13. Matthew 7:3–4.

14. Matthew 18:9.

15. *Webster's New Twentieth Century Dictionary of the English Language, op. cit.,* p. 119.

16. Luke 17:21.

17. Matthew 13:31–32.

18. Matthew 13:33.

19. Matthew 13:44.

20. Charles Fillmore, *Atom-Smashing Power of Mind* (Unity Village, Mo.: Unity Books, 1995), p. 122.

21. John 14:12.

22. Exodus 20:7.

23. Source unknown.

Order—Chapter 7

1. Ecclesiastes 3:1.
2. Song of Solomon 2:11–12.
3. Alexander Pope, "Essay on Man," Ep. IV. L. 49 (from Kate Louise Roberts, *Hoyt's New Cyclopedia of Practical Quotations* [New York and London: Funk and Wagnalls Co., 1922]).
4. Charles Fillmore, *The Revealing Word* (Unity Village, Mo.: Unity Books), p. 56.
5. *Webster's New Twentieth Century Dictionary of the English Language Unabridged*, Second Edition, (Cleveland and New York: The World Publishing Company, 1963), p. 1259.
6. Matthew 6:10.
7. Matthew 9:36.
8. Matthew 14:13–21; Mark 6:32–44; Luke 9:10–17; John 6:1–13.
9. John 2:1–11.
10. Matthew 25:14–30.
11. Matthew 22:37, 39.
12. *Webster's New Twentieth Century Dictionary of the English Language Unabridged*, *op. cit.*, p. 517.

13. *Ibid.*, p. 918.
14. *Ibid.*, p. 1454.
15. *Ibid.*, p. 1729.
16. *Ibid.*, p. 1454.
17. James Dillet Freeman, *The Story of Unity* (Unity Village, Mo.: Unity Books), p. 45.
18. *Webster's New Twentieth Century Dictionary of the English Language Unabridged, op. cit.*, p. 1259.
19. Charles Fillmore, *Dynamics for Living* (Unity Village, Mo.: Unity Books, Selected and Arranged by Warren Meyer), p. 152.
20. Thomas Edison, (from *A Treasury of Great American Quotations*, Charles Hurd, [Chicago, Illinois: J. G. Ferguson Publishing Co.] 1968), p. 209.
21. 1 John 4:7.
22. 1 Corinthians 12:12–26.
23. John Greenleaf Whittier, "Dear Lord and Father of Mankind," *Christian Worship, a Hymnal* (St. Louis, Mo.: Christian Board of Publication; The Bethany Press, 1953), p. 411.
24. Judith Serrin, "Scientist Says God's Existence More Believable," *Dallas Times Herald* (Dal-

las, Texas: Knight-Ridder Newspapers, Saturday, April 1, 1978), p. 6C.

25. Charles Fillmore, *The Revealing Word, op. cit.*, p. 143.

26. 1 Corinthians 14:40.

Creative Expression—Chapter 8

1. Genesis 1:1.

2. Nancy Smith, "From Summit, She Looks to Valley," *Dallas Morning News* (Dallas, Texas: The A. H. Belo Corporation, Publisher, Friday, March 24, 1978), p. 1C.

3. Kenyon Cox, "Work," (from Charles Hurd, *A Treasury of Great American Quotations*, [Chicago, Illinois: J. G. Ferguson-Publishing Co.] 1968), p. 226.

4. Charles Fillmore, *Mysteries of Genesis* (Unity Village, Mo.: Unity Books, 1998), p. 10.

5. *Ibid.*, p. 13.

6. Ralph Waldo Emerson, "Letters and Social Aims. Immortality," (from *Hoyt's New Cyclopedia of Practical Quotations*; Revised and enlarged by Kate Louise Roberts [New York

and London: Funk and Wagnalls Company, 1922]), p. 316.

7. Johannes Kepler, "When Studying Astronomy," (from *Hoyt's New Cyclopedia of Practical Quotations*), p. 317.

8. Charles Fillmore, *op. cit.*, p. 26.

9. Eugene F. Ware, "Whist," (from *Hoyt's New Cyclopedia of Practical Quotations*), p. 454.

10. 1 Corinthians 12:1–31.

11. 1 Corinthians 13:13.

12. Genesis 1:4, 10, 12, 18.

13. Genesis 1:31.

14. Julia Fletcher Carney, "Little Things," (from *A Treasury of Great American Quotations*), p. 160.

15. Ralph Waldo Emerson, "Essays and English Traits," "Circles," (New York: P. F. Collier & Son Co., *The Harvard Classics* [edited by Charles W. Eliot], Vol. V, 1909), p. 155.

16. Psalm 118:24.

17. Mark 10:15.

18. Walt Whitman, "Song of Myself," (from *A Treasury of Great American Quotations*), p. 147.

Divine Discontent—Chapter 9

1. Matthew 5:4.
2. Oliver Herford, "The Chimpanzee," (from Charles Hurd, *A Treasury of Great American Quotations*, [Chicago, Illinois: J. G. Ferguson Publishing Co., 1968]), p. 243.
3. *Collier's Encyclopedia Yearbook*, Covering the Year 1969 (Crowell-Collier Educational Corporation, 1970).
4. *Webster's New Twentieth Century Dictionary of the English Language Unabridged* (Cleveland and New York: The World Publishing Company, Second Edition, 1963), p. 1092.
5. Genesis 1:26.
6. Genesis 3:1.
7. Charles Fillmore, *Metaphysical Bible Dictionary* (Unity Village, Mo.: Unity School of Christianity, 1931), p. 23.
8. Genesis 3:6–7.
9. Genesis 3:14.
10. Charles Fillmore, *Mysteries of Genesis* (Unity Village, Mo.: Unity Books, 1998), p. 54.
11. Genesis 3:15.

12. John 3:14.
13. Original source unknown (from Emma Curtis Hopkins, *High Mysticism* [Cornwall Bridge, Connecticut: High Watch Fellowship]), p. 94.
14. Matthew 5:4.
15. Oscar Wilde, *Woman of No Importance*, Act II (from Kate Louise Roberts, *Hoyt's New Cyclopedia of Practical Quotations* [New York and London: Funk and Wagnalls Co., 1922]), p. 195.
16. Henry Wadsworth Longfellow, "Ladder of St. Augustine," St. 2 (from *Hoyt's New Cyclopedia of Practical Quotations*), p. 344.
17. Francis Quarles, "Emblems," Bk. IV, Emblem 3 (from *Hoyt's New Cyclopedia of Practical Quotations*) p. 21.
18. Ralph Waldo Emerson, "Essays and English Traits," "Compensation," (New York: P. F. Collier & Son Co., *The Harvard Classics* [edited by Charles W. Eliot], Volume V, 1909), p. 89.
19. P. P. Bliss, "Almost Persuaded," *Favorite Hymns*, edited by J. E. Sturgis, (Cincinnati,

Ohio: The Standard Publishing Company, Eighth and Cutter Sts., 1933), p. 174.

20. Theodore Roosevelt, Speech, 1899 (from *A Treasury of Great American Quotations*), p. 231.
21. William Gilmore Simms (from *A Treasury of Great American Quotations*), p. 96.
22. Charles Fillmore, *Christian Healing* (Unity Village, Mo.: Unity School of Christianity, 1968), p. 123.
23. Charles Fillmore, *The Revealing Word* (Unity Village, Mo.: Unity Books), p. 95.
24. Benjamin Franklin (from *A Treasury of Great American Quotations*), p. 42.
25. John 12:32.
26. Psalm 8:4–5.

Free Will—Chapter 10

1. Genesis 1:26.
2. Charles Fillmore, *Christian Healing* (Unity Village, Mo.: Unity School of Christianity, 1968), p. 108.
3. *Ibid.*, pp. 72–81.

4. Charles Fillmore, *The Twelve Powers* (Unity Village, Mo.: Unity Books), pp. 97–109.

5. Charles Fillmore, *Metaphysical Bible Dictionary* (Unity Village, Mo.: Unity Books, 1995), p. 433.

6. Henry Wadsworth Longfellow, "Masque of Pandora," Tower of Prometheus on Mount Caucasus (from Kate Louise Roberts, *Hoyt's New Cyclopedia of Practical Quotations* [New York and London: Funk and Wagnalls Co., 1922]), p. 184.

7. Rosemary Armao, "Blind Deaf Woman Leaves Mental Ward After 19 Years," *The Dallas Morning News* (Dallas, Texas: The A. H. Belo Corporation, Publisher, UPI, Sunday, May 7, 1978), p. 6E.

8. Joshua 24:15.

9. Walt Mason, "The Statesman," (from Charles Hurd, *A Treasury of Great American Quotations* [Chicago, Illinois: J. G. Ferguson Publishing Co., 1968]), p. 242.

10. Doug Domeier, "Cancer-stricken Pets Treated at A & M Facility," *Dallas Morning News, op. cit.*, Monday, January 2, 1978, p. 14A.

11. John 1:1–3.

12. Isaiah 55:11.
13. Charles Fillmore, *Christian Healing* (Unity Village, Mo.: Unity School of Christianity), pp. 68–70.
14. Ella Wheeler Wilcox, "Speech," (from *A Treasury of Great American Quotations*), p. 224.
15. Helen Parmley, "Actors Vary; Play the Same on D-FW Stage," *The Dallas Morning News, op. cit.*, Monday, April 17, 1978, pp. 1, 2A.
16. Ed Timms, "After 13-Year Battle, Goal Attained," *The Dallas Morning News, op. cit.*, Saturday, May 13, 1978, p. 26A.
17. Job 22:28.
18. Francis Cardinal Spellman (from *A Treasury of Great American Quotations*), p. 295.
19. William James (from *A Treasury of Great American Quotations*), p. 202.
20. Jory Graham, "Coming to Terms With the Difficult Choice, Why Me?," *Dallas Times Herald* (Dallas, Texas: Knight-Ridder Newspapers, March 20, 1978), pp. 1, 2B.
21. Charles Fillmore, *The Revealing Word, op. cit.*, p. 197.

Grace—Chapter 11

1. Romans 12:2.
2. Daniel 3:1–18.
3. Daniel 3:17.
4. Daniel 3:25.
5. Daniel 3:26.
6. Charles Fillmore, *Metaphysical Bible Dictionary* (Unity Village, Mo.: Unity Books, 1995), p. 587.
7. Matthew 5:5 (paraphrased).
8. Fillmore, *op. cit.*, p. 444.
9. *Ibid.*, p. 454.
10. *Ibid.*, p. 12.
11. *Ibid.*, p. 82.
12. *Ibid.*, p. 474.
13. Exodus 20:7.
14. Exodus 3:14.
15. Hannah More, "Belshazzar" (from Kate Louise Roberts, *Hoyt's New Cyclopedia of Practical Quotations* [New York and London: Funk and Wagnalls Co., 1922]), p. 268.
16. Source unknown.
17. Matthew 7:1–2.

18. Henry David Thoreau (from *Hoyt's New Cyclopedia of Practical Quotations*), p. 134.
19. Habakkuk 1:13.
20. Genesis 50:20.
21. *Webster's New Twentieth Century Dictionary of the English Language Unabridged* (Cleveland and New York: The World Publishing Company, Second Edition, 1963), p. 1533.
22. Maurice Nicoll, "The Mark" (London: Robinson & Watkins, 1954), pp. 87–112.
23. Romans 12:2.
24. 1 Corinthians 15:51–54.
25. F. B. Whitney & Edna L. Gieselman, "I Behold the Christ in You," *Unity Song Selections* (Unity Village, Mo.: Unity School of Christianity, 1941), p. 221.

Eternality—Chapter 12

1. John 8:58.
2. 1 John 3:2.
3. Abigail Van Buren, "Dear Abby," *Dallas Times Herald* (Dallas, Texas: Knight-Ridder Newspapers, August 11, 1977), p. 18D.

4. Psalm 121:8.
5. Genesis 3:21.
6. Genesis 3:24.
7. John Donne, *Book of Devotions*, Meditation 14 (from Kate Louise Roberts, *Hoyt's New Cyclopedia of Practical Quotations*, [New York and London: Funk and Wagnalls Co., 1922]).
8. Sir Thomas Brown, "Words," Bohn's ed. Vol. II (from *Hoyt's New Cyclopedia of Practical Quotations*), p. 143.
9. *Science of Mind* magazine, issue unknown.
10. Luke 17:21.
11. James Dillet Freeman, *The Story of Unity* (Unity Village, Mo.: Unity Books), p. 211.
12. Luke 12:22, 27–28.
13. Source unknown.
14. *Daily Word* (Unity Village, Mo.: Unity School of Christianity, May 30, 1977).
15. Raymond A. Moody, Jr., M.D., *Life After Life: Reflections on Life After-Life* (Covington, Georgia: Bantam/Mockingbird Book).
16. Matthew 27:57–60.
17. Matthew 28:20.
18. Ralph Waldo Emerson, "Essays and English Traits," "The Over-soul," (New York: P. F.

Collier & Son Co., *The Harvard Classics* [edited by Charles W. Eliot], Volume V, 1909), p. 139.

19. P. P. Bliss, "Wonderful Words of Life," *Unity Song Selections* (Unity Village, Mo.: Unity School of Christianity, 1941), p. 222.

20. Henry Ward Beecher, "Life Thoughts" (from *Hoyt's New Cyclopedia of Practical Quotations*), p. 12.

About the Author

Margaret Pounders is senior minister at Unity Church of Christianity in Dallas, Texas, where she and her husband Frank have served as coministers for more than twenty years.

Ordained as a Unity minister in 1984, Margaret has been a member of several committees of the Association of Unity Churches, which originally published the Activities section for *Laws of Love*. She also has written for *Unity Magazine*.

She was born in Dallas and graduated from Southern Methodist University with a BBA.

Genealogy is her hobby, and she is a member of the Daughters of the American Revolution, Magna Carta Dames, Crown of Emperor Charlemagne, Robert the Bruce Society, and Colonial Dames.

She has a son and daughter and four grandchildren.

Printed in the U.S.A.   147-2245-5M-5-00